THE COLLEGE SUCCESS BOOK

THE COLLEGE SUCCESS BOOK:

A Whole-Student Approach To Academic Excellence

"If you want to feed a man for a day, give him a fish.
If you want to feed him for life, teach him how to fish."

James E. Groccia, Ed. D.

Glenbridge Publishing Ltd.

Cover Illustration
Adam Icenogle

Library of Congress Catalog Card Number: 91-72925

International Standard Book Number: 0-944435-15-7

CONTENTS

FOREWORD

Why are such books as *The College Success Book* needed? There are many answers to this question. First, of the thousands of students entering college each year, approximately 40 percent of them will not graduate. Behind this sobering condition lie many possible causes: lack of enough academic ability to compete; a mismatch between students' characteristics and their chosen major fields of study; low motivation for doing college work; a sense of isolation and not fitting into their college environment; insufficient self-control to cope with the sudden freedom that goes with becoming a college student; family lack of support or even conflict with students' aims and efforts; limited educational preparation; insufficient high-level educational skills (or at least an absence of practicing them—particularly time management, note taking, listening skills and exam-taking skills); and finally, far too little use of the helping resources each campus provides; e.g., academic advisement, tutoring, and counseling. Indeed, it is surprising how few students and their families, when considering colleges to attend, have sought to learn what learning resources and counseling/mental health resources would be available to their sons and daughters should they have need—as many students do.

Many of the these conditions are apt to impact students, especially in their first and second years of college. In contrast, a later cause of attrition is often related to a superior educational preparation that some students bring to college. These students will often perform satisfactorily in the first year, but finding course work easy in their first year can "unfit" them for coping with new materials. This condition is most noted when during the early "easy period" the students have acquired habits that handicap them, especially when the new material demands self-discipline, motivation to learn new material, and higher level educational skills.

Another group of students for whom attrition comes later are those students who, through fear of failure if advanced courses are attempted, continue to register for beginning courses in various fields. In time these students must confront the fact that their academic transcript reveals many credits, but little progress toward a degree. When such students finally take advanced courses, their lack of real preparation to cope with the increasingly complex material places them at a considerable disadvantage.

The above reasons focus largely on the role of the student. But it is only fair to observe that college environments often do not measure up well as facilitating places for students to learn and grow. Fairly common examples include absent, uninterested, passive or erroneous academic advisement; "chilly" classrooms of a few disinterested professors; and sometimes a lack of sufficient support services to provide the help needed by the increasingly diverse students the colleges admit. The predictable inequities for commuting students (in contrast to residential students) are frustrating to many; the wide array of major specialties from which students must select their majors; and finally, pressures to succeed are keenly felt by many students who believe that satisfactory achievement in college is a necessary condition for *any* subsequent employment.

These quite common conditions are some of the reasons why texts such as Dr. Groccia's are needed. Dr. Groccia has had considerable experience in counseling and advising students at a variety of colleges. This book presents the kind of assistance that has proven useful to students. He writes in an attractive, conversational style, providing a holistic approach to enable students to maximize what they can do in college. It is a text useful to all students but particularly beneficial for students taking some form of college orientation/success type course early in their college careers.

Thomas M. Magoon,
Director Emeritus,
Professor Emeritus of Education,
University of Maryland at College Park

INTRODUCTION

Notes

The purpose of *The College Success Book: A Whole-Student Approach to Academic Excellence* is quite simply to provide you with a wide array of skills that will lead to success in college and beyond. You can be taught how to learn, how to develop more effective ways to process the barrage of information coming from all directions. This book will help you learn how to increase productive skills and improve attitudes and behaviors that will guide you through the "information overload" that is characteristic of most, if not all, college settings.

Learning how to learn, having the ability to apply systematic learning strategies and make lifestyle choices that enhance rather than hinder the learning process, is even more critical now in this time of increased technology. The ongoing and evergrowing computer revolution and the resultant explosion of information available to even the average "Joe College" emphasize the need for students to refine their learning processes. It is no longer possible just to memorize simple facts for there are too many of them, and the chances are that with the current pressures for more knowledge they'll be outdated quickly. In fact, it is estimated that half of what a student currently learns in college will be obsolete two and one-half years after graduation.

To maximize the likelihood of academic success, today's college student needs to take an active approach that emphasizes the mechanics of learning and that encourages taking personal control over all the elements available in the learning process. This book focuses on the learning attitudes and behaviors that students can easily grasp and put into action during their academic careers. The goal is academic success; the target is you: what you can (and need) to do to take charge of your own learning.

To make this book "user friendly," I have omitted listing many references and citations in the text itself. All materials used in researching this book are listed in the reference section. I hope this approach increases readability and usability while not compromising scholarship.

The whole-student approach, as illustrated in the title, is unique to this book. There are many study skills books and programs available to college students today. Some even promise straight As or guarantee an

1

increase in your grade point average. I'd love to do that, and although I truly believe that following the suggestions in this book will lead to academic success, I won't make such grandiose claims. I can't control your motivation level, even though I offer helpful suggestions as to how you can. This book will work only if you take the personal responsibility to make it work!

The College Success Book: A Whole-Student Approach to Academic Excellence presents a broad, holistic view of academic life. I believe that behaviors such as exercise and sleep and factors such as diet, stress control, career decision making, and even exposure to sunlight can influence the learning process. These behaviors and factors should be incorporated into an academic success program to maximize its impact. *The College Success Book: A Whole-Student Approach to Academic Excellence* does just this. I want to empower each and every student with every weapon in his or her learning arsenal.

This book is not meant for any one particular type of student. Students vary in the effectiveness of their studying as well as in academic interests and career focuses. Both the good student and the poor student should be able to find something here that will improve their learning skills. The needs of the student who wants a complete studying overhaul, as well as one who desires improvement in only a few study areas, can be met. The chapters are written so that they build upon each other. They follow a logical progression of study behaviors, but each also can stand alone providing assistance with a specific study behavior.

You can use this book in various ways: as a text in an organized study skills course, as a resource in a time-limited academic success workshop, or as a workbook to be used on your own to improve a specific study skill.

When it comes to studying, you *can* teach an old dog new tricks! (Please hold your barks of joy down, as you may disturb your roommate!) Study skills are learned behaviors. Through years and years of practice, repetition, internal and external rewards, you have learned to study the way you do.

A basic law in learning theory states that behaviors that have been learned in the past can be "unlearned" and new behaviors learned in their place. More effective study skills can be learned to replace those determined to be less effective.

It's been my experience that few college students actually have been taught how to study. Many hours have been spent learning math, chemistry, or English, but how much time have you spent learning how to take notes, how to control your study environment, how to concentrate, or how to read a textbook most effectively? In the minds of many people, learning how to study may be like learning how to breathe; it comes naturally with birth and continues to operate automatically until death. This book will attempt to dispel this myth and show you that there are some simple ways to improve your study behaviors leading, it is hoped, to better grades, deeper understandings, and, ultimately, to *academic success!*

Some students may resist learning new study strategies because they believe that they are currently doing all they can. Yet research shows that students tend to exaggerate their use of systematic study techniques and to overestimate the effectiveness of their current study habits.

Effective studying does not mean just spending more time studying. Academic success may be more a result of efficiency of study than of blood, sweat, and tears. The view that college grades generally reflect student effort is not supported. Studies indicate that quantity of study alone may not be enough to ensure academic success. *Students need to learn ways to improve the quality of study efforts, not just work harder or put more time into their studying.*

Another fundamental law of learning is that behavior in part is determined by its consequences. We do what we do partially because of its results. That you are entering or in college indicates that the results of your past and present study patterns have been positive; your study behaviors have led, in some degree, to success. However, that your study methods work does not mean that your studying is maximally effective or that you shouldn't improve your study behaviors. Each college is a unique place and each course a unique experience with special academic demands, traditions, and challenges. Attaining academic success requires that you become flexible in your study habits and learn to modify them to fit new learning environments.

Study skills training programs such as those described in this book have been shown to be effective. Students can learn new study strategies that result in deeper levels of learning, increases in personal growth, and higher grade point averages—all indicators of academic success. *The results are clear: systematic training in academic success skills can lead to academic success!*

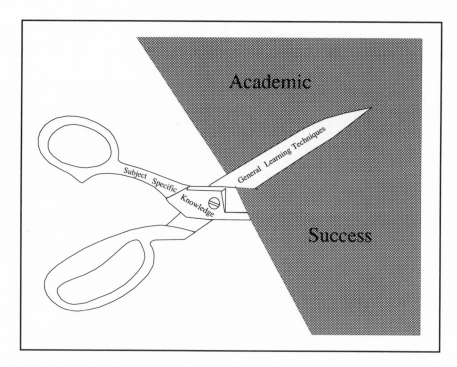

Figure 1. The Two-Pronged Approach (or The Cutting Edges) to
Academic Success

At this point in your study retooling process, it is a good idea for you
to assess your current study behaviors and attitudes. Knowing where you
are before you begin your journey is usually a good idea and can be a way
to determine the specific steps necessary to ensure academic success.

The *Academic Skills Inventory* that follows is designed to measure
study behaviors and attitudes. The feedback provided by this instrument
is not intended to be a scientific, foolproof measure of your study abilities.
Instead, it is a subjective indicator of what you are currently doing—the
good, the bad, and the ugly—in your regular study routine. Once you have
completed the inventory, take a few minutes to review your results. What
trends or patterns do you notice? Are there specific study-skill areas that
seem problematic or in need of special attention?

It is a good idea to repeat this assessment process and to compare
your responses at different times during the school year. Your goal should
be an increase in the frequency and duration of positive study behaviors
and attitudes and a corresponding decrease in the negative ones.

A warning before you begin your journey to Academic Successland: General techniques for effective learning are not sufficient by themselves to ensure academic success. Students must also amass a body of knowledge specific to the subject being studied; learning about learning strategies alone is not enough. Knowledge of how to learn must be applied to gain subject-specific knowledge to produce true academic success. As the illustration in Figure 1 suggests, both blades of the scissors must work together to cut through the tasks required. One blade alone is useful only as a paperweight!

The suggestions that follow present alternatives and options—tips based upon personal and professional experience and educational research. Read, think, analyze, and then decide which, if any, of these tips best fit your needs, abilities, and personality. The responsibility for learning rests on your shoulders. *You*, the learner, not the teacher or the college, are responsible for what you learn. The professor's job is to profess; *the learner's job is to learn!*

ACADEMIC SKILLS INVENTORY

	Rarely or Never	Some- times	Often or Always

A. GENERAL STUDY HABITS & ATTITUDES

1. I approach each course with the attitude that my grade is primarily the result of my effort and ability, not luck or what the professor does

2. I begin each course with the expectation that I will do well

3. I set reachable, realistic goals for each course

4. When determining what to work on first, I write down a list of priorities and start with the most important task

5. I make time for exercise even during the busiest times of the school year

6. I am aware of my eating habits and maintain a balanced diet

7. I have a hard time controlling stress and nervousness

8. I do most of my studying at night and find myself tired in the morning

9. I have a clear sense of what my career is going to be after I finish college

10. I approach each course as unique and develop study plans tailored just for it

11. Before each class meets I spend a few minutes thinking about what will be discussed

12. My study approach emphasizes active involvement— doing as much as I can to learn

	Rarely or Never	Some-times	Often or Always

B. *READING EFFECTIVENESS*

13. I preview the material before reading   _____ _____ _____

14. I read the material to get it finished as quickly as possible   _____ _____ _____

15. I underline, highlight or take notes as I read   _____ _____ _____

16. Immediately after reading, I review and recheck to make sure I understand   _____ _____ _____

C. *NOTE-TAKING*

17. I have trouble anticipating what the lecture will cover   _____ _____ _____

18. I sit in the back half of the classroom   _____ _____ _____

19. I miss important points in the lecture because I'm too busy taking notes   _____ _____ _____

20. I spend a few minutes immediately after class reviewing my notes   _____ _____ _____

D. *TIME MANAGEMENT*

21. My study periods are often too long and I find myself getting bored or easily distracted   _____ _____ _____

22. I write out a study schedule for the entire term so I can see the "big picture"   _____ _____ _____

23. I find it difficult to do work in advance and get caught up in cram sessions to beat the deadline   _____ _____ _____

24. I set up a study schedule that allows me to study every course every day   _____ _____ _____

	Rarely or Never	Some- times	Often or Always

E. *STUDY ENVIRONMENT*

25. I eat when I study

26. Near my desk I have photographs of loved ones

27. I study with a radio or stereo on

28. I study at a place that I reserve for studying only

F. *CONCENTRATION*

29. I find it difficult to block out distractions while studying

30. While studying I think about many things and still get my work done

31. I find it easy to return to studying after taking a short break to clear my head

32. I have a tendency to "daydream" when I study

G. *MOTIVATION*

33. I study to learn as much as I can

34. I study to get good grades

35. I find it difficult to motivate myself to study difficult subjects

36. Getting the highest grade in class is my goal

H. *MEMORY*

37. To remember something, I must repeat it over and over again

	Rarely or Never	Some- times	Often or Always

38. I find it helpful to draw diagrams, outlines, etc., when trying to remember important information   _____ _____ _____

39. My memory for specific facts is worse than for general concepts   _____ _____ _____

40. I use mnemonic learning devices to remember   _____ _____ _____

I. TEST-TAKING

41. I arrive late for tests   _____ _____ _____

42. I expect to do well whenever I take a test   _____ _____ _____

43. Before answering test questions I read all directions and preview the entire test   _____ _____ _____

44. I approach studying for different kinds of tests (e.g., multiple choice, true-false, essay, problem solution, etc.) in different ways   _____ _____ _____

J. MANAGING TEST ANXIETY

45. I get panicky the night before a test and have difficulty sleeping   _____ _____ _____

46. I have difficulty accepting the fact that I might not do well on every test   _____ _____ _____

47. If I get nervous during a test I am able to control it   _____ _____ _____

48. When people finish the test before me, it makes me worry and become more tense   _____ _____ _____

K. WRITING SKILLS

49. I begin working on my research papers as soon as possible to avoid end-of-the-term cramming   _____ _____ _____

50. I know how to use the library and can quickly find information that I need   _____ _____ _____

	Rarely or Never	Some-times	Often or Always
51. I follow a set format and structure when writing an essay or paper	_____	_____	_____
52. When writing I have a tendency not to footnote as much as I should	_____	_____	_____

PART ONE

GENERAL FORMULA FOR ACADEMIC SUCCESS

Chapter 1

THE FORMULA:

$$AS = (D + H + N + S + F) A_1 A_2$$

Studying can be considered a combination of behaviors that are engaged in only periodically under special conditions, the object of which is to increase learning, knowledge, and performance. *Webster's Third International Dictionary of the English Language, Unabridged (1981)* defines studying as "the application of the mind to the acquirement of knowledge through reading and reflection, observation, or experiment" (p. 2268).

The process of acquiring knowledge does not take place in a vacuum. Your body does not stop functioning nor does your life come to a screeching halt when you study. Studying is one behavior among many in which you engage, and all of these behaviors are interrelated to form the reality of YOU. Focusing exclusively on the intellectual aspect, studying, and excluding attention to your other needs and behaviors will result in inefficient learning outcomes.

I believe that you can improve your study behavior and academic outcomes by adopting a holistic, general approach to studying. This means developing a view of studying as being one of many interconnected behaviors and attitudes in which one can be engaged simultaneously. Each of these behaviors and attitudes impacts on the quality of your study performance and must be incorporated into your general study plan.

The many different factors that contribute to successful studying have been drawn together into what I call the General Formula for Academic Success (Figure 2). The general formula can be stated as: *Academic Success (AS)* is the product of the sum of *Self-Discipline (D)* plus *Good Health Habits (H)* plus *Attending to your Nonacademic Needs (N)* plus *Awareness of Learning Style (S)* plus *Flexibility (F)* multiplied by *Anticipation (A_1)* and *Action (A_2)*. $AS = (D + H + N + S + F) A_1 A_2$. Don't be afraid of this formula; it's really quite simple. I will describe each part and provide exercises that will help you to understand it clearly. Keep this illustration handy for reference as you read along.

$$AS = (D + H + N + S + F)\, A_1\, A_2$$

	D Self-Discipline	**H** Positive Health Habits	**N** Focus on Meeting Needs	**S** Styles of Learning	**F** Flexibility	**A₁** Anticipation	**A₂** Action
AS Academic Success	Accept control and responsibility	Exercise regularly	Recognize nonacademic as well as academic needs	Recognize factors that influence learning	Approach each course as unique	Preview work to do	Do something, don't be a passive learner
Good study habits	Adopt a positive mental attitude	Eat well		Determine preferred learning conditions	Tailor study behavior to fit each course	Don't be surprised	Question, repeat, recite, take notes, do study problems, underline, highlight, etc.
Good grades	Self-Awareness (Strengths and weaknesses)	Get enough sleep	Early career planning			Plan ahead and review	
Academic success	Set realistic, attainable goals	Maximize light			Review study schedule regularly		The more you do, the easier it becomes to encode into memory
Career success	Learn to set priorities	Learn to control stress				Learn how to create advanced organizers	
Personal fulfillment							Use multisenses
Nirvana!							

Figure 2. General Formula for Academic Success: $AS = (D + H + N + S + F)\, A_1\, A_2$

Each specific component in this general formula deserves a detailed explanation. Read each carefully and complete the exercises as you go. There is a great deal of information contained in this section, so take your time and proceed at a relaxed pace. *Before beginning, however, it may be helpful to preview all of Part One.* Take a few minutes, flip through the pages, and take notice of the words in BOLD type, italics, illustrations, and the exercises included. Don't do them yet; just get a feel for what's to come. This previewing method is an important element in effective reading and will be described in greater detail in Part Two, Chapter 3.

Chapter 2

General Formula for Academic Success

$$AS = (\underline{D} + H + N + S + F)\ A_1A_2$$

PRACTICE SELF-DISCIPLINE (D)

By self-discipline I mean a combination of behaviors and attitudes that focus your attention on accepting responsibility for and controlling the events, priorities, and goals of your life (as much as is realistically possible).

Practicing self-discipline means accepting control and responsibility. Develop the attitude that you make things happen in your world. You are not a puppet on a string being pulled and tugged by forces beyond your control. Academic success should be thought of as a result of ability and effort more than as an outcome of luck or difficulty of task. If you adopt this attitude, you may increase positive outcomes through attention to what you really can influence (e.g., effort) rather than what is beyond your control (e.g., luck). Luck or the difficulty of a test is rarely under our direct control, but how well we study for that test is.

Focusing on what we can control requires self-discipline, acceptance of our own responsibility, and not looking for excuses or scapegoats for poor performance. The use of "I" statements as opposed to "he" or "she" statements can signal a shift in thinking indicating acceptance of responsibility. Practice telling yourself things such as "What *I* get on this test is a result of how well *I* study," or "*I* have the ability to learn this stuff," or "*I* got an A on that term paper."

Practicing self-discipline means adopting a positive attitude. The power of positive thinking has been described in the popular as well as the scientific press. Specific expectations about one's ability to perform specific tasks influence the decision even to attempt the task as well as how persistent and, consequently, how successful at that task one will be. Researchers have found that positive feelings about one's ability to be successful can be useful in predicting future successful school performance. Attitudes and expectations do, in fact, influence outcomes.

15

Studying with a positive view of one's ability and an expectation of positive results increases the likelihood of actually getting positive results. Of course, positive attitudes will not by themselves influence future achievement unless adequate skills and appropriate incentives to perform the necessary tasks are present. Success won't be guaranteed by positive attitudes, but if you can increase the *probability* of success, why not do it?

Remember the children's story about the little engine that could. He kept telling himself that he could deliver the train full of toys over the mountain to the waiting children in the valley. Even though a larger engine failed before him, he kept saying, "I think I can"—and guess what? He did!

Say the following sentence five times out loud to yourself right now (don't worry about what your roommate will think): "I am going to learn more and get better grades this term." Repeat this or some other statement that creates a positive expectation of success every day, before every test, or whenever you start to study. Listen to what you say and soon you will do it!

Practicing self-discipline means knowing yourself. Take a few minutes to find a quiet place and focus on who you are and what your strengths and weaknesses are. Think about your abilities and the areas that need development.

Complete the following exercise, focusing on both the positive and negative aspects of your academic and intellectual abilities. List your strengths and weaknesses when it comes to school and then go back and put a star (*) beside the most important characteristic in each column.

Strengths   Weaknesses

1.   1.

2.   2.

3.   3.

4.   4.

5.   5.

Before proceeding, take another moment or two to reflect upon your lists. Any surprises? Now take an additional few minutes and tell yourself that your goal is to capitalize on your strengths and minimize your weaknesses. The exact ways to do this may not be readily apparent at this time, but a key strategy is to begin a positive mind set now—a mind set that focuses on your strengths rather than on your weaknesses. Your new level of confidence will help you reach new levels of achievement.

Self-awareness can be attained in many ways. The exercise that follows can reveal interesting information about who you are. A student counselor at your college would be a helpful resource for assisting with a more in-depth discussion of exercises of this type.

Write down the first response that comes to mind. Don't contemplate or try to analyze your responses until you are finished. Be honest with yourself; answer candidly. You don't have to show your answers to anyone else, but you may find discussing them with others helpful.

SELF-AWARENESS INVENTORY: UNFINISHED STATEMENTS

There are many avenues you can travel to seek self-awareness and understanding of who you are. Take a few more minutes and complete the unfinished statements below.

I am at my best_____

My school work _____

I'd be happy if _____

My friends think I'm _____

My teacher _____

Sometimes I worry about _____

What I like best to do _____

If I could change school I'd_____

My advisor thinks I'm _____

If I could change myself I'd _____

My parents think I'm _____

I wish I could be more_____

When I grow up I want to _____

If I had three wishes_____

The reason I am in college is _____

After college I_____

Studying makes me_____

When faced with an important test I _____

My motivation to do well is _____

I concentrate best when _____

   Now review your responses. Does anything surprise you? Could you, in a few sentences, describe this person? Can any of your responses influence how you study? Use this space below to write down your responses.

This inventory is not intended to provide an in-depth analysis of your personality, but it can be useful to trigger some thought and introspection. The more you know about yourself—the more you understand your goals, abilities, and interests—the more directed, motivated, and energized you will become to pursue your college education.

Practicing self-discipline means setting realistic short- and long-term goals. Everything flows from goals. Figure 3 illustrates how goals form the foundation upon which work behavior is built.

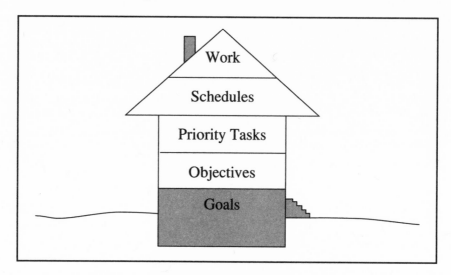

Figure 3. Goals Form a Foundation for Work

Knowing what you want in terms of attainable short- and long-term goals provides direction and motivation. The goals become targets to aim for and gauges by which to measure your progress. Take a few minutes and jot down some of these goals as they exist right now. You define what "short" and "long" mean; e.g., 1 week, 1 month, 1 semester; 1 year, 5 years, 10 years.

Short-Term Goals   Long-Term Goals

1.   1.

2.   2.

3.   3.

4.   4.

5.   5.

I believe that students can benefit greatly from assessing goals often. Ask yourself about your goals frequently—at the beginning of each academic term and whenever doubts about college crop up.

Practicing self-discipline means planning and setting priorities. Sorting through the immediate demands of living can help you balance your academic, social, and personal responsibilities. *Setting priorities means to determine when, how, and in what order you will do what you need to do.* One way of ordering priorities is to fill out a "To Do" list such as the one that follows.

To Do List

	Task	Priority Level	Done
1.	_____	_____	_____
2.	_____	_____	_____
3.	_____	_____	_____
4.	_____	_____	_____
5.	_____	_____	_____
6.	_____	_____	_____

In the column marked "Task" list a number of things that you must do; e.g., homework assignment, papers, tests to study for, notes to recopy, laundry to do, calls to make, pages to read, etc. You may choose to do a new list for each day or for one week at a time. If you are just beginning to use this prioritizing method, I recommend that you start on a daily basis.

Once you have completed this list, you will need to assign a priority rating to each task. This is the critical part of the process. I suggest that you use three levels of importance when setting priorities—*must* do now, *should* do soon, can *wait* until later. You can use numbers (1, 2, 3) or letters (A, B, C) to represent these three levels of importance. Or try using different-colored pens or pencils, such as red to indicate a hot, top priority; and blue, a cool, low priority. This rating will tell you what you need to attend to first. *Always start with your highest priority tasks, those assigned an "A" or a "1."* As you finish a task, put a check (√) mark or write in the date of completion in the "Done" column. Try to finish all of your top-level tasks before you move to the "B" or "2" level. If you redo your lists on a daily basis, "B" level priorities may move up to "A" level, remain the same, or even move down to "C." Learn to reevaluate your assignments and needs on a regular basis and prioritize accordingly. You become the manager of your individual work force!

<u>Remember:</u>

- Planning, making choices, and prioritizing is not easy. Be prepared to experience some difficulty.

- Planning is more than just thinking about what you want to do.

- Planning means making decisions as to what, when, and how.

- Planning is making lists and setting priorities.

- Planning means action and follow-through.

Chapter 3

General Formula for Academic Success

$$AS = (D + \underline{H} + N + S + F) A_1 A_2$$

MAINTAIN POSITIVE HEALTH HABITS (H)

Notes

College students live a daily paradox in the ivy-towered halls of learning. An argument can be made that you are at the pinnacle of your physiological potential, the zenith of your biological life, and the high point of your health capacity. Strength, speed, endurance, physical functioning are all at levels that may be unsurpassed at any future time in your life. The paradox is that despite (or maybe because of) this high-level functioning, your general health behaviors may be at their all-time lows. The combination of behaviors such as unhealthful eating, sleeping, exercise, stress management, and the ingestion of chemicals (alcohol and/ or other drugs) frequently indicates an abusive, negative lifestyle.

College students typically do not attend to the maintenance of good, healthful, or wellness-oriented lifestyle behaviors. They often drink too much, exercise infrequently, sleep irregular hours, study into the early morning hours, experiment with drugs, and eat foods with questionable nutritional value. Thank goodness you are at the high point of your physiological capacity—it may be the only reason you survive the college years!

As you will soon realize, general health habits play an important role in learning and influence academic outcomes. Therefore, you may find completing the following Lifestyle Fitness Survey (adapted from *Health Style - A Self Test,* U.S. Department of H.H.S. Publication No. [PHS] 81-50155) worthwhile. This is not a pass/fail type of test but simply a mechanism to tell you how well you're doing in order to stay healthy. The areas covered by the self test are those to which most health experts recommend Americans pay attention. The test provides a good introduction to understanding the importance of positive health habits in relation to academic success[1].

---

[1]Note: People with special health conditions should see physicians before implementing any changes in eating habits or physical exercise activities.

23

Lifestyle Fitness Survey[1]

Cigarette Smoking	Almost Always	Some-times	Never

If you never smoke and no one sharing your immediate living environment smokes, enter a smoking score total of 10 and go on to the next section.

	Almost Always	Some-times	Never
1. I avoid smoking cigarettes.	4	1	0
2. My roommate/spouse avoids smoking.	2	1	0
3. I smoke only low tar and nicotine cigarettes or I smoke a pipe or cigars.	2	1	0
4. I avoid smoking when I study.	2	1	0

Smoking Score: _____

Alcohol and Drugs

	Almost Always	Some-times	Never
1. I avoid drinking alcoholic beverages or I drink no more than 1 or 2 drinks a day.	4	1	0
2. I avoid using alcohol or other drugs (especially illegal drugs) as a way of handling stressful situations or the problems in my life.	2	1	0
3. I am careful not to drink alcohol when taking certain medicines; e.g., medicine for sleeping, pain, colds, allergies.	2	1	0
4. I read and follow the label directions when using prescribed and over-the-counter drugs.	2	1	0

Alcohol and Drugs Score: _____

[1]Adapted from Health Style - A Self Test, U.S. Department of Health and Human Services Publication No. [PHS] 81-50155.

Eating Habits	Almost Always	Some-times	Never
1. I eat a variety of foods each day; e.g., fruits, vegetables, whole grain breads & cereals, lean meats, dairy products, dry peas & beans, nuts & seeds.	4	1	0
2. I limit the amount of fat, saturated fat, and cholesterol I eat (including fat on meats, eggs, butter, cream, shortenings, organ meats; e.g., liver).	2	1	0
3. I limit the amount of salt I eat by cooking with only small amounts, not adding salt at the table, and avoiding salty snacks.	2	1	0
4. I avoid eating too much sugar (especially frequent snacks of sticky candy or soft drinks).	2	1	0

Eating Habits Score _____

Exercise/Fitness			
1. I maintain a desired weight, avoiding over- and underweight.	3	1	0
2. I do vigorous exercises for 15-30 minutes at least 3 times a week; e.g., running, swimming, brisk walking, aerobics.	3	1	0
3. I do exercises 15-30 minutes at least 3 times a week that enhance muscle tone; e.g., yoga, stretching, isometrics, weight lifting.	2	1	0
4. I use part of my leisure time participating in individual, family, school, intramural or team activities that increase my level of fitness; e.g., volleyball, bowling, golf, baseball.	2	1	0

Exercise/Fitness Score: _____

Stress Control	Almost Always	Some-times	Never
1. I enjoy school.	2	1	0
2. I find it easy to relax and express my feelings freely.	2	1	0
3. I recognize early, and prepare for, events or situations likely to be stressful for me.	2	1	0
4. I have close friends, relatives, or others whom I can talk to about personal matters and call on for help when needed.	2	1	0
5. I participate in group activities (e.g., church, school organizations) or hobbies that I enjoy.	2	1	0

Stress Control Score: _____

Safety	Almost Always	Some-times	Never
1. I wear a seat belt while riding in a car.	2	1	0
2. I avoid driving while under the influence of alcohol or other drugs.	2	1	0
3. I obey traffic rules and the speed limit when driving.	2	1	0
4. I am careful when using potentially harmful products or substances; e.g., household cleaners, poisons, electrical devices.	2	1	0
5. I avoid smoking in bed.	2	1	0

Safety Score: _____

Your Lifestyle Fitness Scores

After you have figured your scores for each of the six sections, circle the number in each row that matches your score for that section of the test.

Cigarette Smoking	1	2	3	4	5	6	7	8	9	10
Alcohol & Drugs	1	2	3	4	5	6	7	8	9	10
Eating Habits	1	2	3	4	5	6	7	8	9	10
Exercise & Fitness	1	2	3	4	5	6	7	8	9	10
Stress Control	1	2	3	4	5	6	7	8	9	10
Safety	1	2	3	4	5	6	7	8	9	10

There is no total score for this test. *Consider each section separately.* You are trying to identify aspects of your lifestyle that you can improve in order to be healthier, to reduce the risk of illness, and to increase your general learning ability.

What Your Scores Mean to YOU

Scores of 9 and 10

Excellent! Your answers show that you are aware of the importance of this area to your health. More importantly, you are putting your knowledge to work for you by practicing good health habits. As long as you continue to do so, this area should not pose a serious health risk. Since you scored very high on this part of the test, you may want to consider other areas where your scores indicate room for improvement.

Scores of 6 to 8

Your health practices in this area are good, but there is room for improvement. Look again at the items you answered with a "Sometimes" or "Never." What changes can you make to improve your score? Even a small change can often help you to achieve better health.

Scores of 3 to 5

Your health risks are showing! It is important for you to change these behaviors.

Scores of 0 to 2

Your answers show that you may be taking serious and unnecessary risks with your health.

If you scored below 9 on sections of the preceding health survey, you might benefit from information about how and why to change your lifestyle behaviors.

Here are some specific suggestions for maintaining good health habits:

Exercise regularly

Make exercise a regular part of your day. A positive relationship has been shown between regular physical fitness training and the improvement of mental functioning (especially during and after physical stress), reduction of work-related errors, improved work performance and work attitudes, improvement in feelings and mood states, and a general improvement in self-concept. If you don't exercise regularly, start now! *(Caution: Before engaging in any program of physical activity, you should consult a physician and have a thorough physical exam.)*

To experience the positive effects of exercise, experts recommend working out a minimum of twenty minutes a day, three times a week. An activity such as running, walking, swimming, biking, cross-country skiing, or other aerobic activity that gets your heart rate to 70-75 percent of maximum and keeps it there for at least twenty minutes should be repeated at least three times per week.

The following steps will help you to compute 70 percent of your maximum heart rate:

Step 1:

Males = 220 - your age = maximum heart rate
Females = 220 - your age x 1.5 = maximum heart rate

Step 2:

Figure your resting heart rate. (The normal range for most people is between 70-80 beats/minute.)

To find resting heart rate, sit up in bed when you first awake in the morning and count your heart beat for 6 seconds, then add a zero; e.g., 7 becomes 70.

If your heart rate is below 70, the formula in Step 1 must be modified to:

Males = 220 - # beats below 70 - age
Females = 220 - # beats below 70 - age x 1.5

If your resting heart rate is above 80, modify Step 1 to:

Males = 220 + # beats above 80 - age
Females = 220 + # beats above 80 - age x 1.5

Step 3:

Subtract your resting heart rate from the maximum and multiply the remainder by .70. (If you smoke, are 20 pounds overweight, have had surgery or a serious illness, multiply by .65.)

Step 4:

Add this product to your resting heart rate. Do most of your physical fitness exercise so your heart rate will reach this figure after you have been working out for a few minutes.

Step 5:

Check your heart rate periodically by checking your pulse for 6 seconds and adding a zero. If you are tired at 70 percent, don't push it; slow down. Getting your heart rate above the 70-75 percent range may not have any positive effect on your physical fitness, so don't overdo it.

Try to achieve an exercise pace at which you can carry on a conversation with another person. Remember to give yourself a chance to warm up before and cool down after exercising, and don't use exercise as a way to avoid studying!

Eat well

"Eat a balanced diet." I am sure that you have heard this suggestion many times, enough that you have effectively learned to ignore it. Without sounding too paternalistic, I strongly urge you to pay attention to what you eat and to recognize the direct connection between diet, nutrition, your brain, and your behavior.

Research in brain activity, nutrition, and behavior has pointed to a clear biochemical link between food and the functioning of the brain. In studies using animal and human subjects, learning has been shown to be affected by the presence or deficiency of minerals such as aluminum, zinc, and iodine.

Two recent books, *Managing Your Mind and Mood Through Food,* by Dr. Judith Wurtman (1986), and *Eat Right, Be Bright*, by Arthur Winter, M.D. and Ruth Winter (1988), provide provocative arguments for the influence of food on mood and performance. In addition, Dr. Wurtman suggests a dietary plan called "Power Eating" that enables the individual to tailor eating habits in order to produce certain desired mental effects.

The following summary and synthesis of these authors' findings should provide tangible suggestions on how best to eat to produce mental alertness and focused concentration—two mental functions essential to learning. Because of the newness of this area of research, I will go into more technical detail than I have with other sections. (*Caution: This information is not intended to substitute for the advice of a physician. Please consult with your medical doctor in all matters relating to your physical health.*)

The research done at MIT by Dr. Wurtman and her colleagues points to a clear relationship between food, mood, and performance. In most basic terms, certain foods influence the production and function of chemicals in the brain. These chemicals are responsible for carrying messages in the brain and are called neurotransmitters. These neurotransmitters affect the way the brain works and result in differing levels of mental activity and mood.

Three of these chemicals—dopamine, norepinephrine and serotonin—are produced or influenced directly by the food that we eat, and their levels in the brain are controlled by our dietary intake. Dopamine and norepinephrine are known as the alertness chemicals; serotonin, the calming chemical, based on their effects on brain activity.

The brain synthesizes these chemicals from the amino acids contained in food. The principal amino acid responsible for the production of the alertness chemicals is tyrosine. Tyrosine is found in food high in protein. The amino acid from which the chemical serotonin is made is tryptophan. Tryptophan is found in foods high in carbohydrates, such as sugar and starch.

Eating foods high in protein will increase the production of tyrosine. During periods of increased activity, your brain rapidly uses up its supply of dopamine and norepinephrine. The added tyrosine from protein will produce additional amounts of these alertness chemicals. The result is an increase in mental alertness, quickness, energy, and attention. Therefore, *choose foods high in protein and low in fat and/or carbohydrates when you want to become more active, motivated, and mentally alert*—such as when beginning to study for a big exam.

Eating carbohydrates alone, without protein, allows tryptophan to reach the brain in greater quantities, where it is used to produce serotonin. This results in a greater sense of calm, relaxation, ability to handle stress, and ability to concentrate. *Choose foods high in sugar or starch and low in protein and fat to increase your ability to concentrate and control anxiety*. This may be advantageous in test-taking situations or when trying to learn complicated, detailed material such as technical, mathematics-oriented subjects.

A couple of words about foods high in fat: *avoid them*! Foods high in fat are the most difficult for your stomach to digest. During the long digestive process, blood is diverted to the stomach and away from the brain. The result is a slowing down of mental processes and, thus, inefficient thinking. Fat is higher in calories than other foods and is associated with heart disease and other significant health problems. In general, stay away from high-fat foods such as butter, hard cheeses, mayonnaise, fatty meats and creamed soups. High fat always means high calorie, high risk, and low performance. (Skip the butter on your popcorn tonight!)

The following are lists of foods from which you can choose to produce the desired mental states.

Alertness, Motivated State of Mind (Proteins)

Best:
    Chicken (with skin removed)
    Fish
    Shellfish

Veal

Lean beef (all visible fat removed)

Good:

Dried peas and beans

Lentils

Low-fat cottage cheese

Low-fat yogurt

Skimmed or low-fat milk

Tofu and other soybean foods

Relaxation, Concentration, Focused Attention (Carbohydrates)

Sweets (simple carbohydrates):

Candy

Cookies

Cake

Ice cream

Jelly, jam

Pie

Soft drinks

(This runs counter to popular mythology and advertising claims. Eating a candy bar will *not* give you a sudden burst of energy—just the opposite will happen!)

Starches (complex carbohydrates):

Bread (rolls, bagels)

Crackers, muffins

Pasta

Potatoes

Rice

Cereal (without milk)

Dr. Wurtman's research indicates that three to four ounces of protein and one to one and one-half ounces of carbohydrates are enough to produce the desired mental effects. However, individuals 20 percent or more over ideal body weight and women just prior to menstruation may require two to two and one-half ounces of carbohydrates for relaxation and focused concentration to occur. Megadoses of artificial substitutes or supplements have not been proven to have beneficial effects and should be avoided.

Food can also be used to influence and manipulate our natural biological clock that controls mental energy levels throughout the day.

Figure 4 illustrates how one's individual mental energy peaks within hours of awakening and then slowly declines toward the end of the day.

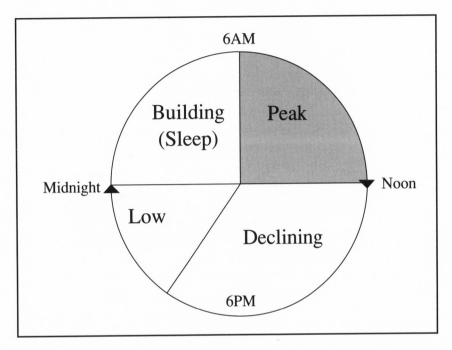

Figure 4. Biological Energy Levels.

This biological clock (called circadian rhythms) repeats itself every twenty-four hours and is similar for all people. Mental and physical energy levels are greatest from about 6:00 a.m. to noon, and it's at this time that the potential for effective learning and academic performance is at its peak. These circadian rhythms are very strong, but they can be manipulated and altered. Some people do this through gradual learning processes; they train themselves to work late night and early morning hours (and even convince themselves that they enjoy this).

By following a planned eating program one can override natural biological rhythms and produce high energy and focused concentration when they are most productive and rewarding. Here are some general eating tips that may easily be applied to improve study effectiveness.

Eat a good breakfast. Getting food into your system at the time your body is shifting into high activity after a night of rest provides a natural boost, allowing you to get into full swing more quickly and effectively. Eating a nutritious breakfast also discourages you from overeating at lunch. Overeating results in calorie overload, which can lead to mental and physical lethargy.

Avoid midmorning snacks. Academic activity is one form of mental activity that is adversely affected by added calories that come in the form of most snack food. The exception to this rule is that if your breakfast is less than adequate or if you get up *very* early, you should have a nutritious snack to prevent an all-out lunch binge.

Lunches should be high in protein and low in fat and calories. Lunch comes right when your natural internal energy levels are beginning their major declines. If academic attention is required in the afternoon, your lunch should be high in protein. Foods high in fat and calories produce an energy drain and should be avoided. Eat lightly at lunch as a general rule.

Avoid afternoon snacks if you've eaten a good, nutritious lunch. If you are bored or need a break from studying, go for a walk or do some light exercises, but *don't* attack the refrigerator or rush for the snack bar.

If you need to study or work in the evening, you should eat a dinner that will counteract the natural slowdown that occurs at the end of the day. Choose foods high in protein and low in fat and carbohydrates if you need to be productive and mentally alert. Keep the evening meal light, as a large dinner speeds up natural biological slowdown. If you must have carbohydrates with your meal, eat them after eating some protein; this will kick the energizing chemicals into action first, thereby minimizing the calming effects of the carbohydrates.

When you want to relax after studying and need rest before a big exam, eat an evening meal high in carbohydrates and eat it in a relaxing environment and relaxed manner. A "Big Mac" or "Whopper" with large fries at the local fast food hangout is not exactly what I have in mind. A plate of pasta and a slice of bread would do just fine. Eat a moderate amount and you can even have a few chocolate chip cookies as a final reward!

Caffeine can be used to improve mental performance. Caffeine has a stimulating effect on the brain and produces quicker thinking and reaction time, greater accuracy and alertness, and longer attention span. Therefore, a cup or two of caffeinated coffee or tea in the morning will get you going and mentally ready for studying. The stimulating effect of coffee lasts for three or more hours for most people, making the midmorning coffee break unnecessary.

Also, a cup of coffee at 3:00 or 4:00 in the afternoon will probably provide a positive boost for most people. An even better idea is a cup of coffee preceded by a sweet roll or pastry. (Life can be rough!) The carbohydrates in the latter create a sense of focusing and calming down; then the caffeine kicks in and elevates your mental energy level so you can continue to study until dinner.

Dr. Wurtman recommends avoiding caffeine after this midafternoon snack unless you need to stay alert in the evening to study or to finish an important project or report. Caffeine is found in coffee, tea, cola beverages, and cocoa in differing amounts, and college students have been known to drink them all.

Learn to manage stress and anxiety

College life can be fraught with deadlines, tests, oral and written presentations, and other stress-inducing stimuli. Anxiety can severely and negatively affect academic, social, and personal performance.

It may be helpful for you to get a picture of the level of stress that you currently are experiencing.

Examples of some high stress events that are not uncommon for college students to experience include:

Death of a parent
Parent's divorce
Serious illness or injury to yourself, close friend or family member
Flunking out of college
Failing an important test or course
Loss of financial aid
Unwanted pregnancy
Break-up of a relationship
Being placed on academic warning or academic probation
Conflict with a roommate or professor

In addition to these high-stress events, college life is filled with many everyday stressors. College students are not immune from the problems of living faced by others. These everyday problems by themselves may not cause you undue stress, but when taken together, can be extremely uncomfortable and anxiety producing.

I recommend that you consider learning some form of relaxation or stress management strategy.

Simple yet effective stress management techniques are readily available. Figure 5 is a list of stress-reduction techniques identified by college students. Try some out; it's easier than you think to reduce and control stress.

- meditation	- hobbies
- exercise	- health spas
- time management training	- change jobs
- study breaks	- social support
- listening to music	- self-confidence training
- humor	- drop annoying acquaintance
- faith	- ceremonies and traditions
- self-help groups	- vacations
- hypnosis	- biofeedback
- encounter groups	- diet changes
- psychotherapy	- reorder priorities
- variety	- Yoga
- writing	- relaxation response
- drawing/art	- Shavasan
- assertiveness	- altering work loads training
- deep abdominal breathing	

Figure 5. Suggested Stress Reduction Techniques

Note: Sources of stress are highly variable. What is stressful to one may not be to another. It follows that stress reduction is also highly variable. What works for one does not necessarily work for everyone.

For those of you who desire more specific suggestions on how to control stress, the following relaxation techniques may prove helpful. The use of self statements has proven successful for many students in achieving states of calm, relaxation, and reduction of stress. The process is not difficult to practice. Get yourself into a comfortable position free from distraction and interruption. Read over the instructions before you try them out. You might even try reading them out loud and recording them on your tape recorder. Play back your recording and follow your own instructions.

Relax Your Body: Take time to visualize, imagine, and feel the relaxation of each part of the body as you silently repeat the following phrases; then just "let go":

I feel quiet. I am beginning to feel quite relaxed. My feet, my ankles, my knees and my hips feel heavy, relaxed and comfortable. The whole central portion of my body feels relaxed and comfortable. My neck, my jaws, and my forehead feel relaxed. They feel comfortable and smooth. My whole body feels quiet, comfortable, and relaxed.

Calm Your Feelings: As you remain comfortable and relaxed, use the following phrases in the same manner as above, visualizing, imagining and feeling the warmth:

> My arms and hands are heavy and warm. I feel quiet. My arms and hands are relaxed, relaxed and warm. My hands are warm. Warmth is flowing into my hands; they are warm . . . warm. My hands are warm . . . relaxed and warm.

Calm your Mind and Turn Attention Inward: On each phrase imagine and feel the quietness and withdrawal of the attention inward:

> I feel quiet. My mind is quiet. I withdraw my thoughts from the surroundings and I feel serene and still. Deep within myself I can visualize and experience myself as relaxed, comfortable, and still. I am alert but in an easy, quiet, inward-turned way. My mind is calm and quiet. I feel an inward quietness.

Maintain the inward quietness for about two minutes. Reactivate by taking five slow, full breaths. Stretch and feel energy flowing through your body.

Get enough sleep

Students are notorious for staying up late and sleeping late. "All-nighters" are not uncommon for many students. Your dorm may be a hotbed of activity at 1:00 a.m.—hall sports, loud stereos, card games, telephone calls, study sessions, bull sessions—all of which, for most people, are incompatible with sleep. (Woe unto those unfortunate souls with 8:00 a.m. classes!)

Getting enough sleep may be dependent upon two different strategies. *First,* you may have to take a more active approach to stimulus or environmental control. You may have to ask people to be quiet, or request that the semester-long floating card game relocate to someone else's room, or ask your roommate to use his earphones while listening to his latest CDs.

The *second* strategy depends more upon your ability to use personal control or different time-management strategies. *Late-night studying can be minimized by learning how to distribute your study throughout the day, not waiting until the last minute.* Discovering your "lost hours" (time spent watching TV or "sacking out" during the afternoon between classes) during which you can study may free up more evening hours for that mysterious behavior called sleep. Part Two, Chapter 2 focuses on time management in greater detail, so you might want to preview it at this time.

Although there is no general theory to explain how sleep loss affects information processing ability, the physiological, psychological, and performance effects of sleep loss have been well-documented. These effects are even more pronounced when performance tasks are prolonged, inherently boring, or lacking in immediate incentives (like studying and most college exams!).

It would seem that academic performance would certainly suffer after prolonged periods of sleep loss such as those resulting from "all-nighters." There is evidence, however, that given the proper motivation, students can overcome these negative effects by consciously trying harder. Increased effort can significantly improve performance for short periods of time.

So if you must lose sleep preparing for that critical exam or presentation, don't lose hope also. You can still pull it off successfully with much extra effort. I would not recommend, however, that this become your typical study pattern because of the documented negative cumulative effects of sleep loss on the brain and the superiority of efficient studying over intensified cramming.

Don't abuse drugs

Normal functioning of the brain and the central nervous system enables you to pick up this book, turn its pages, focus visual attention and, most importantly, decipher the meaning of the printed words and encode this meaning into memory. The brain controls the action of billions of nerve cells throughout the body, enabling thought and action to take place. One's learning, in fact all of one's behavior, is the result of the brain's interpretation of incoming, and management of outgoing, nerve impulses. These impulses can be significantly altered—depressed, intensified, or distorted— by the chemical activity of drugs.

Drugs act upon the basic elements of the brain such as nerve cells and neural transmission sites and upon the specific areas of the brain involved in the learning process and memory. Alcohol and other drugs do not enhance mental functioning. They negatively affect the brain's ability to process and store information.

This seems like knowledge that everyone possesses, right? Right. However, the participation in midweek or weekend "partying" is a fact of life for a number of college students. Become aware that alcohol and other drugs ingested do play a role in your learning and subsequent academic performance and act accordingly. I'm not suggesting that you necessarily jump on the abstinence bandwagon, but recognize that what you drink or ingest on Wednesday night may reduce your study effectiveness on Thursday and, subsequently, your test score on Friday's exam.

Get enough light

An emerging area of research has focused on the treatment of seasonal mood depression with concentrated exposure to full-spectrum lights. The popular notion of "cabin fever" (feelings of irritation and low energy as a result of being indoors during long periods of bad weather) may actually be an accurate reflection of seasonally influenced depression caused by lack of exposure to full-spectrum daylight. The exact physiological reasons and responses behind this emotional reaction are still unknown. However, these effects have been well-documented. The evidence regarding effects of extended exposure to light (within certain light spectrums) is mounting.

It has been demonstrated that children and adolescents who regularly had difficulty during winter months with irritability, fatigue, sadness, sleep disturbances, and irregular school performance, as well as depressive symptoms, reversed these symptoms and improved mood and social functioning after a course of light therapy. This finding is of special interest because it touches briefly on our chief concern, academic performance.

No research to date has directly explored the effects of light exposure on studying, resolving academic difficulties or academic performance enhancement. However, I would like to take a calculated risk and propose that you may benefit by applying the research from this emerging field to improving learning and academic behavior.

I suggest that you attempt to *maximize your exposure to full-spectrum daylight* in hopes of positively influencing your academic success. Studying is certainly influenced by mood, and positive, nondepressive feelings are more likely to contribute to one's study efforts. Feelings of well-being and happiness would seem to contribute to effective studying compared to those of depression and sadness.

I would like also to suggest the following specific study behaviors:

1) Study during a.m. rather than p.m. (This should have even greater impact upon study effectiveness considering natural energy highs during this time of day.)

2) Move your desk in front of a window if you can.

3) During the winter term make extra efforts to get outside during the day.

4) Exercise during the a.m.

5) Purchase a full-spectrum light and install it in your desk lamp or somewhere in your room. (Contact personnel at your college/ university counseling center for names and addresses of suppliers. Full-spectrum lights are also sold at some natural food stores and garden display retailers.)

Chapter 4

General Formula for Academic Success

$$AS = (D + H + \underline{N} + S + F)\ A_1 A_2$$

ATTEND TO YOUR NONACADEMIC NEEDS (N)

Recognize the importance of social, personal, spiritual, and interpersonal growth. College provides unique opportunities to learn social skills and to establish meaningful relationships. There's more to college than the three R's. *The key here is striving for and attaining balance between your academic and nonacademic needs.* Any time-management plan you follow must recognize and allow time for socializing and personal development. One-dimensional scheduling focusing only on your schoolwork will not only make "Johnny a dull boy" but also will result in frustration and eventual discarding of the schedule altogether.

Attending to your nonacademic needs means early and continuing career development planning. Don't wait until your junior or senior year to begin to plan for your career. Start developing a "grand plan" early and focus on how individual courses and out-of-class activities can be integrated into it.

Students who are pursuing identified majors and following career paths find it easier to adjust to the academic, social, and emotional demands that come with college life. Better adjusted students have higher grade point averages, graduate on time more frequently, are selected for more student leadership positions, and are generally more involved in campus activities than students who are less well adjusted.

Therefore, if you are undecided as to your major, it may be to your advantage to begin to obtain information about majors, careers, and your own interests and abilities early in your college career. Being able to focus on a major, even if you change it later on, may make the adjustment to college easier and future academic success more easily attainable.

The two exercises that follow will be helpful to students who feel some indecision concerning what to major in at college. The first exercise

41

asks you to reflect back to high school as a way to help you identify your academic interests and strengths.

High School Interests and Strengths Survey

Step 1: Think back to the courses you took in high school. In Column A list the subjects you *liked* best. In Column B list what it was that you liked about that subject.

Column A	Column B
Example: Math	I enjoy solving problems

_____   _____

_____   _____

_____   _____

_____   _____

_____   _____

Step 2: Now think about the courses in which you *did* best. List those courses in Column C. In Column D describe what you learned to do in that subject.

Column C	Column D
Example: Science	Conduct experiments

_____   _____

_____   _____

_____   _____

_____   _____

_____   _____

Step 3: Reflect upon your out-of-class activities. In Column E list those activities that you *enjoyed doing* (whether or not they were school sponsored). In Column F describe what it was that you liked about that activity.

<u>Column E</u>   <u>Column F</u>

Example: Hiking   Being with nature

_____   _____

_____   _____

_____   _____

_____   _____

_____   _____

Step 4: Take a few moments to review steps 1, 2, and 3. Are there subjects that appear in more than one column? Are there any common elements to subjects that appear in the columns? Do your out-of-class interests relate to any of the subjects that you enjoy or do well in? Can you think of any college majors that are similar to subjects that you enjoyed and in which you did well in high school? Write your answers to these questions in the space that follows.

_____

_____

_____

_____

_____

_____

The second exercise focuses on your knowledge and use of the resources on your college campus. If you are undecided or concerned about choosing a major, take a few minutes to find answers to the following questions.

Major Selection Survey

Who could you talk with on your campus about academic majors? Include the names of other students, resident advisors, professors, academic advisors, career and personal counselors.

_____

_____

_____

Where are the Career Counseling Center and Academic Advising Center on your campus?

_____

_____

_____

What services are available for students on your campus to help them choose majors?

_____

_____

_____

List the names of people who are working in the field that you are considering as a major that you could talk with for information about careers. Include parents, friends, relatives, professors, alumni, etc.

_____

_____

_____

What is the next step you need to take in order to select a major? When will you take it?

_____

_____

_____

Most colleges provide career development seminars or personal career counseling at the advising, career, or counseling centers. Attend these seminars and use the resources available to you. Some institutions have computer-assisted career guidance programs that provide novel and exciting approaches to choosing a major and selecting a career path. Your college counseling or career center may have this new high-tech career resource available; contact the center and find out.

Having career goals helps provide direction and focuses your attention on attainable outcomes of the educational process. Knowing where you are going with your academic program, in terms of clear goals, helps stimulate and maintain motivation. Motivation has been shown to be a critical component of academic success. Therefore, clarifying your career goals can result in immediate as well as long-term gain.

Recognizing nonacademic needs also means attending to the spiritual part of your life. The college years are a time when students typically ponder "the big questions," such as "What is the meaning of life?" "Is there a God?" "What values do I hold as essential to my life?" This process of searching for meaning is what the spiritual dimension of life is about. I am not necessarily equating spiritual needs with organized religion but use this term to represent the many diverse ways that people enrich their inner spirits.

Recognizing and attending to spiritual needs can greatly influence the quality of your college experience. For example, choice of a major and a career can be closely connected to a person's life goals and spiritual values. If you do not know what is important to you, these choices may become more difficult to make. On the other hand, clarity about why you have chosen a life path can provide motivation and energy to devote to the hard work it takes to get there. Engaging in study or hard work that conflicts with personal and spiritual values can cause anxiety, procrastination, and poor performance. Congruence between values and vocation may increase performance and provide a sense of fulfillment.

Attending to your spiritual needs may help you to weather the stresses and emotional storms of academic and college life. In keeping an eye on "the big picture" (e.g., life, purpose, values, love, relationships, meaning, etc.), day-to-day pressures and deadlines can be seen for what they are rather than as matters of life-and-death importance.

Focusing on spiritual needs often fosters a sense of community, a joining together with others who share your values, beliefs, and concerns. This social support network may be most helpful and can facilitate the development of meaningful relationships that can be called upon in times of crisis. This social support may be even more important to help you through those everyday problems and demands common to life in college.

Chapter 5

General Formula for Academic Success

$$AS = (D + H + N + \underline{S} + F) \, A_1 A_2$$

BECOME AWARE OF YOUR LEARNING STYLE (S)

What are your learning needs? How, when, where do you learn best? People react differently to different learning conditions. "Learning style" is the term used to indicate that each student has his or her own unique way of responding to different environmental and personal conditions when trying to learn.

When beginning to study, one should first consider all the factors that will influence learning and attempt to set up a situation that best fits with one's preferred learning style.

The *Learning Style Check List* that follows can be used to help determine how you best like to learn. Take a few minutes to complete this list as best you can. Check each item that corresponds to the way you like to learn or the situation in which you are the most comfortable while studying.

Learning Style Check List

Check which of the following relate to you:

Environmental Conditions

1. Need quiet

   Can tolerate sound

   Need noise

2. Require warm place

   Require cool place

48

3. Need bright light

    Need low light

4. Require desk and chair

    Require comfortable, lounging furniture

Motivational-Emotional Factors

1. Self-motivated

    Unmotivated

    Other-motivated

2. High level of internal, self-control

    High level of external, other-control

3. High persistence—"stick-to-itiveness"

    Low persistence—easily distracted

4. Prefer internal, subjective rewards

    Prefer external, tangible rewards

5. Need highly structured learning conditions; e.g., specific assignments

    Need little structure; e.g., self-paced independent instruction

People and Social Contact Factors

1. Prefer to study alone

    Prefer to study with one friend

    Prefer to study with two or more friends

    Prefer to study with adults

    Prefer combination of alone and with others

Physical Characteristics and Needs

1. Prefer learning by listening

    Prefer learning by seeing

    Prefer learning by touching

    Prefer learning by doing

2. Require food while studying

    Do not require food while studying

3. Function best in early morning

    Function best in late morning

    Function best in afternoon

    Function best after dinner

    Function best in late evening

    Function best after midnight

4. Prefer to remain in one place while studying

    Prefer to move about while studying

When finished, review your responses. Answer the following questions:

1. What have I learned about my learning style?

    _____

    _____

    _____

2. Is there anything about my learning style that needs to be changed?

    _____

    _____

    _____

3. How can I find ways to use my learning style to my advantage?

    _____

    _____

    _____

4. Is my learning style best suited for learning in my present academic situation?

    _____

    _____

    _____

5. What changes can I make in my study plans?

    _____

    _____

    _____

Learning efficiency and study effectiveness may be improved when these learning-style factors are taken into account. In addition, teachers who develop teaching/learning strategies that allow students to work within their diagnosed learning styles can enhance pupil learning effectiveness. Maybe you should consider becoming an educational reformer and sharing this information with your professors?

Awareness of your learning style would be helpful when beginning to study and may be extremely useful when setting up your study schedule. This checklist is not intended to be a scientific determination of your learning style but, rather, a helpful means to become aware of the ways in which you like to learn. This information about yourself then can be used to determine the most effective study plan—tailor-made for your unique learning style.

Chapter 6

General Formula for Academic Success

$$AS = (D + H + N + S + \underline{F})\, A_1 A_2$$

BE FLEXIBLE (F)

Notes

It's been my observation that many students get locked into study habits that become ritualistic. What I mean is that students don't necessarily study a certain way because it represents the most effective approach. They do it that way because they always have done it so. Studying becomes a rigid series of habits performed lockstep without much analysis or concern for the unique requirements of the material to be learned.

Break out of this rut! *The general concept of flexibility suggests that you allow the unique features of each course, each test, each professor to determine your study behaviors.* Instead of imposing your "tried and true" but not necessarily most efficient or effective study rituals blindly, analyze what behaviors are appropriate and plan your study attack accordingly.

Just because studying a certain way worked in high school does not guarantee success in college. "All-nighters" in history might get you an A, but calculus might require a different study strategy to produce the A. Differing types of exams, such as multiple choice, essay, problem solutions, call for different types of knowledge that may be gained in differing ways. *Be flexible.* Prepare a study plan for each course in a way that confronts the unique features of each course.

You also should consider your own personal strengths and weaknesses in this planning process. If you know you are weak in one area, such as math, allocate more time and resources to counter that weakness. Also, capitalize on your strengths as much as possible. Answering the following questions may be helpful in planning your study attack. Do this for each course at the beginning of each term or semester.

53

Questions To Ask To Determine Your Study Plan

1. Professor

    A. Have I had a class with him/her before? _____

    B. What is his/her class presentation style (lecture, discussion, etc.)?
       _____

       _____

    C. Does he/she have regularly scheduled office hours? _____
       If so, when? _____

    D. Do I feel comfortable talking to this professor, asking questions?
       _____

    E. Are there other instructors (TAs, lab assistants, etc.) I could go to
       for help? _____

2. Course Requirements

    A. How are grades determined? _____

    B. What types of exams will be given? _____

    C. Term paper/project? Specific requirements? _____
       _____

       _____

    D. Labs—when, what kind of reports required? _____
       _____

       _____

    E. How involved in course presentations should I be? _____
       _____

    F. Is homework required? _____

    G. Does class attendance count? _____

3. Schedule

    A. When does class meet? _____

    B. Will course require library or computer access? _____

    C. When should I study? _____
       _____

    D. When can I schedule review/preview times? _____
       _____

    E. How do I need to modify my present study/work schedule? __
       _____

    F. How must I alter my extracurricular activities? _____
       _____

4. Study Behaviors

    A. Do I need to work alone or can I work with study group of other
       students? _____

       _____

    B. Where can I study (my room,library, etc.)? _____
       _____

5. Previous Experience

    A. How knowledgeable am I about course content? _____
       _____

       _____

    B. Have I taken similar courses in the past? _____
       _____

       If so, what worked best, what didn't work out so well? _____
       _____

       _____

       _____

Review your responses before proceeding. How can this information be used to develop a study plan that will be maximally effective? Are your courses all the same? Will you need to individualize your study plan for each course?

Chapter 7

General Formula for Academic Success

$$AS = (D + H + N + S + F)\underline{A}_1 A_2$$

LEARN TO ANTICIPATE WHAT IT IS THAT YOU WILL BE LEARNING (A_1)

Plan ahead. I do not think that much effective learning occurs in random, disorganized ways. Nor does much learning occur by surprise. Being prepared and primed to anticipate what is coming is critical to my approach to studying. Anticipation helps to make new information meaningful because you already have begun the process of mentally connecting it with previously learned material.

Anticipation forces thought, analysis, and a sense of expectation that can be validated or modified by direct experience. Structure and organization of new knowledge is facilitated. Your mind becomes like an organized file cabinet containing folders with labels on them. Future retrieval is easier from this file cabinet than from a mind that resembles a cluttered desk top with paper and folders scattered here and there.

Anticipation is an advanced organizer or a preview of coming attractions. Your appetite is whetted; you are ready for more; you have a sense of what's coming, and you have begun to consider what you might do with it. Anticipation helps you form a mental index into which material can be more easily and neatly stored and retrieved (remembered).

The concept of anticipation permeates almost every chapter in this book. Specific examples of anticipation (such as reviewing your lecture notes before class or previewing the entire chapter before you begin to read) will be described and elaborated upon.

In a sense, anticipation (and the next component, action) are more important than the other elements of my general formula for academic success. I suggest that you read these two sections again and again throughout your time with the book.

Chapter 8

General Formula for Academic Success

$$AS = (D + H + N + S + F) A_1 \underline{A}_2$$

BE ACTIVE (A_2)

Unless new information is placed in a structured pattern, unless you do something with it that allows it to make sense to you, it will quickly be forgotten. You must do something besides passively read for learning to be maximized. Don't just sit back listening to your teacher. Remember, *it is your responsibility to learn, not the teacher's responsibility to make you learn. Professors are paid to profess; your job as a student is to actively study and learn. Think, question, repeat, recite, take notes, do study questions, underline, highlight, form study groups, draw diagrams, complete review questions, quiz yourself orally—the more active you are, the more sense modalities you use, the easier it will be to encode new information into your long-term memory banks.*

Take a few moments now to review the general ideas presented in Part One. As a means to encode the General Formula for Academic Success into memory, complete the following diagram in as much detail as possible. Use your own words whenever possible. Then refer back to Figure 2 to see how you did.

$$AS = (D + H + N + S + F) \quad A_1 \quad A_2$$

PART TWO

ACADEMIC SUCCESS SKILLS

Chapter 1

UNDERSTAND AND INCREASE YOUR MOTIVATION

Motivation in a general sense is that which influences the arousal, selection, direction, and maintenance of all human behavior. This chapter will focus on one type of motivation, the motivation to learn. Students require some form of stimulus to activate, provide direction for, and encourage persistence in their study and learning efforts. *Motivation is this energy to study, to learn and achieve and to maintain these positive behaviors over time.* Motivation is what stimulates students to acquire, transform, and use knowledge.

Many psychologists believe that behavior is purposeful and functional, that we do certain things because the consequences somehow meet our needs. This idea underlies the concept of motivation, and it is basic to our understanding of learning and studying. *People study and learn because the consequences of such behavior satisfy certain internal and/or external motives.*

Studying is influenced primarily by your desire for and attempts to satisfy personal and social motives. These are the real energizers for studying. You study to satisfy natural human curiosity and desire for new ideas and knowledge as well as to attain social status, approval, affiliation and acceptance by friends, parents, and significant others. Studying is also motivated by your need to not flunk out (security) and because it makes you feel good about yourself to do well (self-esteem).

Knowing this is great, but you probably are wondering how you can improve your motivation to study in practical, real ways. The following pages offer some suggestions. Some are general, some specific. Your ability to apply these tips will depend upon your capabilities for self-control and your own values concerning different approaches to motivation.

Suggestions to Increase and Improve Motivation

1. *Establish a learning-oriented environment.* Students tend to view schoolwork as something to be done to get something, to receive credit. Academic work is often viewed as a means to an end (a degree)

and not as an end unto itself. Although this approach is certainly appropriate, it may not be sufficient to ensure academic success. I would encourage you to attempt to change your studying to make learning and knowledge valued outcomes in and of themselves.

An environment that is learning oriented has several key features. Students in this atmosphere expect and intend to learn. While at college, focus your attention and energies on learning. Make learning your number one priority. Socializing and recreational activities, although important and not to be ignored, should take a back seat to learning.

Learn to expect good things about yourself, your teacher, and the learning process before each class starts. Psych yourself up; don't accept negative evaluations of your courses or your professors before you even begin. Give the professor room to fulfill your positive expectation for the course and his or her behavior, and this might add to your academic performance.

Approach each course with a *positive mental attitude* that indicates that you intend to learn and intend to be successful. This attitude will help you concentrate on and attend to the academic tasks at hand. A positive mental attitude also increases the probability of positive results: intending to learn increases the likelihood of learning.

2. *Learn to recognize and capitalize on your intrinsic interests and natural needs for competence, curiosity satisfaction, and achievement.* The term "intrinsic" refers to the self-rewarding characteristic of an activity; engaging in that certain activity is worthwhile for its own sake. No reward is sought or expected from this activity. You may play a game, read a book, or complete a project for the sake of doing it, not for some expected result.

Interest is learned; so is disinterest. Motivation to learn and to study a certain subject may be improved by stimulating your interest in that subject. It may be difficult to get terribly excited about "Differential Equations" or "Philosophy 101," but try to find some aspect or application of it that captures your interest.

Humans by nature are curious creatures. Curiosity can be defined as an internal tendency to explore new stimuli or ideas. New experiences, ideas, people, and places appeal to this sense of curiosity. Allow your curiosity free reign. Explore new ideas; seek new experiences. Approach each course with a sense of curiosity. Expect new discoveries; be prepared "to go where no man has gone before."

Develop a questioning attitude that stimulates this natural curiosity as you begin each new course. Don't view a course as a closed system of facts but, rather, as a body of new information with challenges and mysteries that await discovery.

The *natural, internal human need to deal effectively with one's world describes our need for competence.* As infants we explore, crawl, grasp, listen, touch, and eventually learn to walk and talk. We have a need to become proficient in controlling and mastering our environment. College students have a higher level of this need for competence, and that need provides energy to learn and to achieve. The desire for self-improvement is a strong motive for students, and translating this need into action is a necessary requirement for academic success. This natural need for competence can be a powerful motivation to study.

3. *Set and attain realistic goals.* Goal setting can become a useful motivational strategy for various reasons. *First,* setting a goal involves an intention to achieve and thereby serves to facilitate learning. *Second,* it directs your attention and behaviors toward the desired goal. *Third,* it gives you the opportunity to experience success—provided, however, that you set attainable, realistic goals.

This last point deserves clarification. *Effective goals are specific rather than general.* Specific goals are those in which the outcomes are clearly identified and attainable within some realistic time frame. General goals are long term, while specific goals are achievable in the short term. Specific goals must also fall within your range of abilities. Try as I may, I doubt that I would be able to achieve my specific goal of playing for the Boston Celtics—given my size, age, and terrible jump shot!

Setting clear, short-term goals, and checking your progress toward attainment of them, offers constant immediate incentive for performance. The result is greater persistence in the target behavior—studying. The motivational benefit of setting short-term, attainable goals is probably of greater importance in private, out-of-class study situations, wherein specific measures of learning are less clear and feedback (i.e., test results) is usually infrequent and delayed.

Try setting and attaining goals during a specific time interval such as a day, week, or term. Determine objectives that you will try to satisfy in each course at the beginning of the term. Your teacher will often include a list of course objectives in the course syllabus. Look closely at these; can you tie them into other goals that you have set for yourself? Use the goals as targets to shoot for or as a road map providing direction to your intended destination: increased learning, an A, a degree, etc. Setting specific short-term goals may enhance more than academic achievement. Your natural interest in studying may also be stimulated as your perception of success and achievement is increased.

4. *Take initiative in your learning.* Initiative means self-control and self-regulation of learning activities. It implies voluntary rather than forced studying and means developing a sense of personal causation for one's behavior. Learn to view success or failure as resulting from your actions rather than as being controlled or manipulated by other persons or other external causal factors.

People learn to attribute success or failure to one or more of four basic elements: *ability, effort, task difficulty,* or *luck.*

Students high in motivation to achieve tend to view their effort and ability as the most important factors in determining all outcomes. Persons low in achievement motivation tend to feel that success is only weakly influenced by how hard they work (effort). They attribute failure to lack of ability. Students who see lack of ability as the cause of their failures expect to repeat failure because one's ability is thought of as a stable characteristic; it varies little over time—either we're smart in math or not, and practice will lead to only slight improvement. Students with this fatalistic orientation may avoid future opportunities to learn and may fail to reach their fullest potentials.

The belief that success is the result of factors such as ease of test, teacher bias, or luck does not motivate a student to make future efforts to succeed nor to believe in his/her ability to be successful. Attributing success to factors that are within one's power to control (e.g., time spent studying or number of review problems completed) increases motivation to work harder to succeed.

Do not assume that if you do poorly in one semester, or in one subject, that you will continue to do so in the future. Convince yourself that if the appropriate effort is invested (not just in terms of time but, rather, in use of effective study habits), the chances of academic success are greatly improved.

You can learn new ways of thinking about what causes your academic success or failure. Some possible ways in which this may be done include:

a. *Experience success.* Capitalize on your strengths. Take some courses in which you have a high likelihood of doing well. *Success builds success. Start with easy courses and work up to hard courses.* Challenge yourself with difficult tasks after you have succeeded with the easier ones.

Success or failure by themselves may be less important than your perceptions of the causes of the success or failure. Success builds feelings of self-competence only if the student accepts responsibility for that success. You must experience success, but you must also learn to see the positive relationship between your behavior and your performance and accept the responsibility for success. You also need to remember that effort and persistence can overcome failure.

b. *Give self-feedback. Keep telling yourself that your success is a result of ability and effort,* not just a result of ease of task or luck. Focus on factors that are directly under your control. At the same time, convince yourself that failure is the result of poor effort.

c. *Develop a positive mental attitude.* Develop an attitude built upon the power of positive thinking. You can *expect success* based upon past success and upon your abilities and effort. Tell yourself that failure is not permanent and does not have to be repeated—things will get better with effort!

d. *Recognize when you need to increase effort, when you need to overcome underdeveloped abilities.* Don't put yourself down if you perceive that you may have difficulties in a course because you haven't yet acquired the skills or knowledge to be successful. Isn't that why you are taking the course in the first place? Use this knowledge to stimulate effort rather than feeling frustration and giving up. Give yourself instructions before these courses, in fact, before all courses, that emphasize the importance of effort in achieving success. Be flexible in determining the level of effort necessary for each course, as each is different and may call for different degrees of "blood, sweat and tears."

5. *Encourage and get informative feedback and external control as necessary.* You need feedback from others to guide your goal-directed activities. Use your professor as the main source of outside feedback. Don't rely solely on her scheduled feedback; i.e., exams. Periodically seek out your professor with questions that will give you information on how well you are doing, how well you are grasping the new material. Use your professor's scheduled office hours; ask for oral and

written feedback and for tips on how to overcome errors. These efforts should contribute not only to effective learning; they may lead your professor to recognize your effort and thereby color his subjective feelings about you. At grading time this may prove advantageous in final student evaluations. Certainly, in courses where student participation and effort is rewarded by your professor, active pursuit of feedback may be helpful.

6. *Use reinforcement principles to increase motivation. In some situations, the use of tangible rewards might be helpful to improve, increase, or maintain good study behaviors.* How often, how hard, and how long you study may be influenced by what happens after the studying. If your studying is followed by a pleasurable reward or positive consequence, such as a candy bar or an A, the chances that you will study in the future are increased. On the other hand, if you receive punishment after studying (other students call you a bookworm or geek for studying when they are partying or you fail your exam), the likelihood of future studying is decreased.

You may be able to increase your motivation to study, especially in low-interest courses, if you arrange for a reward to follow some set period of study. Reward yourself with a candy bar or a carrot stick for reading ten pages of physics, for example. The more rewarding a behavior is for you, the easier it will be to do it, and the harder and longer you will tend to work at it.

Use of reinforcement principles may lead to increased motivation to study. Following is a list of suggestions that may help improve your studying through the application of rewards.

a. *The first step in learning to systematically use external rewards to increase motivation is to specify what is rewarding for you.* Make a list of possible rewards or payoffs that you can give yourself after studying. Make a list of rewards before studying and have those rewards available when you finish. Use different types of rewards so you don't tire of one thing. Rewards lose their positive value if overused.

This questionnaire lists things and experiences that you may be able to use as rewards for productive studying. Circle the degree of pleasure that each item provides as a means of identifying potential rewards.

Reward Questionnaire[1]

	Very Pleasurable		Neutral		Not at all Pleasurable
Eating					
Fruit	1	2	3	4	5
Candy Bar	1	2	3	4	5
Ice Cream	1	2	3	4	5
Nuts	1	2	3	4	5
Celery/Carrot Stick	1	2	3	4	5
Chips	1	2	3	4	5
Cookies	1	2	3	4	5
	1	2	3	4	5
Drinking Beverages					
Water	1	2	3	4	5
Soft Drink	1	2	3	4	5
Coffee	1	2	3	4	5
Tea	1	2	3	4	5
Beer	1	2	3	4	5
Wine	1	2	3	4	5
	1	2	3	4	5
Other					
Listening to Music	1	2	3	4	5
Working Crossword Puzzles	1	2	3	4	5
Watching TV	1	2	3	4	5
Playing Sports	1	2	3	4	5
Reading	1	2	3	4	5
Attending Movies	1	2	3	4	5
Singing	1	2	3	4	5
Dancing	1	2	3	4	5
Hiking/Walking	1	2	3	4	5
Running/Jogging	1	2	3	4	5
Lifting Weights	1	2	3	4	5
Aerobics	1	2	3	4	5
Playing Cards/Games	1	2	3	4	5

[1]Reproduced with permission of authors and publisher from J. Cautela and R. Kastenbaum, "A Reinforcement Survey Schedule for Use in Therapy, Training, and Research," *Psychological Reports* 20 (1967): 1115-30.

Shopping	1	2	3	4	5
Gardening	1	2	3	4	5
Sleeping	1	2	3	4	5
Taking a Bath/Shower	1	2	3	4	5
Talking to Friends	1	2	3	4	5
Helping Others	1	2	3	4	5
Making Love	1	2	3	4	5
Going to Church	1	2	3	4	5
Praying	1	2	3	4	5
Building Models	1	2	3	4	5
Working on Your Car	1	2	3	4	5
Playing Instrument	1	2	3	4	5
_____	1	2	3	4	5
_____	1	2	3	4	5

b. *Learn to reward yourself after studying for some predetermined time or after finishing a certain number of problems.* Never reward before, always after studying.

c. *When learning a new behavior or studying a low-interest subject, begin with a high reward-to-work ratio.* In other words, if you don't particularly like calculus or you find it very difficult, reward yourself frequently for small amounts of study.

d. As you learn to study this low-interest subject, *gradually increase the amount/time of studying done to earn your reward.* Increase the studying as you decrease the frequency of reward.

e. *Gradually shift to an intermittent reward schedule as your studying improves.* This means that you move from rewarding yourself every time you study to every other or every third time. In this way you decrease your dependence on the tangible reward as your motivation to study. It is hoped that at this time the work will start to pay off with better grades. (A slot machine works on an intermittent reward schedule and is quite effective at motivating people to take chances at winning.)

f. You can *increase your motivation to study a hard or less preferred course by studying it before you study an easier or more preferred course.* You will feel a heightened sense of accomplishment by getting the more difficult one out of the way, and the second course takes on the form of a reward for a job well done.

g. *It's more motivating and productive to make a reward contingent or dependent upon an amount of work accomplished rather than on time spent studying.* Rather than reward yourself for an hour of study, reward yourself for pages read or problems solved.

h. *It may be motivating for you to keep a chart or record of what you have accomplished.* This becomes a form of *feedback* that will be reinforcing.

i. *It may be more helpful when studying to compete with yourself rather than to compete with others.* Try to keep bettering your previous grades rather than to focus on the performance of others. Your performance is under your control; you cannot control how well others do, how much effort they put into a course. Therefore, your chances of success with yourself are much higher than they would be when competing with others.

Applying these principles of reinforcement together with the other general motivation tips discussed in this chapter should get you energized and directed toward higher levels of academic success. High levels of motivation to achieve may, in fact, be *the* critical element in your study repertoire that puts you "over the top." The pages of history are full of stories of individuals who through drive, determination, and motivation overcame hardship, physical or intellectual difficulties, or environmental handicaps to achieve unparalleled levels of success. A measure of this success may be within your grasp also if you can make these motivation suggestions part of your life.

Chapter 2

ORGANIZE AND SCHEDULE YOUR TIME

Notes

Nobody has enough time, yet everyone has all there is. A major factor contributing to poor academic performance for many students is poor time management. Time itself is not the problem. *We* are the problem or, more accurately, *the villain is our inability to manage time so that we can achieve maximum output with minimum input.*

I am sure that all of you at one time or another have attempted to set up a schedule to organize your study time and, possibly, your life in general. What most of you have probably found is that schedules, like New Year's resolutions, are meant to be broken. I used to spend the first few days of each academic term setting up my "foolproof" schedule and then the remaining weeks of the term changing it. I don't think that my failure was due to the unworkability of schedules themselves but was, rather, the result of my rigidity and compulsiveness in setting up the schedule. I usually condemned my schedule to failure by compulsiveness and by trying to overorganize my whole life. I have found that many students who try setting up a schedule also fall into this overscheduling trap and give up time-management attempts in frustration and confusion.

I have now developed an approach to successful scheduling that incorporates planning *and* flexibility—flexibility that allows for change and spontaneity, planning that enables me to determine my goals and priorities and to schedule my activities so I can successfully accomplish those goals.

Some people resist scheduling because they feel that it restricts their freedom; it locks them into a regimen that is enslaving. I believe that a good schedule increases rather than decreases freedom. It allows you to do what you have to when it needs to be done—in its own planned time and space—thereby providing uninterrupted freedom to do other things. I don't think it's indicative of freedom to have to pass up some desirable social event because you have to cram for an exam that you've known about all term. Nor are you free when you have to hand in a paper that you know is below your usual quality level because library and reference materials were not available at the end of the term when you wrote it.

Personal freedom depends upon the ability to plan, schedule, organize and control your time, not to be a slave to last-minute studying, deadlines, and crisis-management lifestyles. You control your studying with effective scheduling; it doesn't control you!

Let's try to make scheduling and time management simple and workable. *Here are nine tips for effective scheduling and time management.*

1. *Review your learning style and take this into account when developing a study schedule.*

    Reread the section on learning style and review your responses to the *Learning Style Check List*. Ask yourself if there is anything about your preferred way of learning that can be reflected or included in your study schedule.

    It may also be helpful at this time to review the information in Part One, Chapter 2 concerning internal biological rhythms. Most people are naturally more energized during the first few hours after waking up in the morning. It seems obvious that you should consider capitalizing on this natural biological energy and set up a study schedule that has time for important study early every day. Radical as it seems, you can study before as well as after classes!

    If you think that you are a "night person," someone who is most productive in the evening or early morning hours, you may in fact have learned to alter your biological rhythms. You may have learned to change your internal energy clock, possibly expending much effort to do so. Consider changing into a "day person" for a few weeks and see if your studying and academic performances change. Doing so will also expose you to additional full-spectrum sunlight, improving your emotional outlook as well.

2. *Determine your general needs and goals.*

    Before you begin to prepare a schedule, rethink your academic and nonacademic goals and needs. In addition to your need to pass Calculus II this term, consider what you want to accomplish in the social, personal, and physical aspects of your life. Think in terms of both the short and long run. Be realistic.

    Too often students get carried away in their scheduling for studying and schoolwork and leave no time for necessary social activities, recreation, or relaxation. They quickly become resentful of the rigid schedules and abandon them feeling, rightfully so, that they are impossible to keep.

Review Part One, Chapter 3 at this time. Take a few minutes to complete the following *Goals and Needs Survey*. The purpose of this survey is to help you focus on the "whys" and "how comes" of your academic pursuits. For it to be effective, your study schedule must factor in time for you to address all your needs, not just the academic needs.

The following *Goals and Needs Survey* may help you identify academic as well as nonacademic priorities.

GOALS AND NEEDS SURVEY

Why am I here at college?

What do I want to be doing in five years, ten years?

What do I want (need) in terms of a personal relationship?

What are my short-term goals for this term, this quarter, this semester?

     - academic

     - personal

     - social

     - physical

What special social activities do I want to attend or participate in this term, this quarter, this semester?

3. *Determine the specific goals and requirements for the academic term.*

Figure out the objectives and work demands specified by each instructor for each course. What are the reading assignments, projects, exams, problem sets, homework, and papers, and when are they required to be finished? Think in terms of "due dates" or deadlines for completion of course requirements. Once deadlines are determined, work backwards to schedule the appropriate time to do what needs to be accomplished by the due date.

Goals should be specific, achievable, have target dates, and have measurable outcomes. People who have specific goals achieve more in less time and are more challenged and motivated to get things done.

4. *When setting up your schedule, utilize all sources of information available.*

Consult your course syllabus, term activities calendar, "What's Going On" column in your school newspaper, the calendar printed on the inside cover of the yearly *Undergraduate Catalog*, sports schedules, any and all other resources containing dates and times of activities.

5. *Spread work out over the entire term.*

As much as possible, utilize the entire amount of time available to you during each academic term. Each term, quarter, or semester has "crunch" times, but you may be able to avoid some or ease the pressure by spreading out work into any "slack" time available. People learn more effectively if they can spread their studying out into smaller, more widely spaced practice periods than if they try to learn big chunks of material in short, condensed blocks of time. In other words, studying small amounts daily works better than does cramming or pulling an "all-nighter."

6. *Don't forget computer access needs.*

Computer and word processing needs at college can occasionally get pretty heavy. You probably are aware of horror stories describing computer or word processing centers with long lines that reach into the early hours of the morning. If you need to use these technological resources, plan ahead as much as possible. Ask the coordinator or student monitors when user traffic is the lightest and schedule your time accordingly.

7. *Prioritize.*

Learn a system to help you recognize the importance of what needs to be done. As tasks are completed, this should be reviewed and modified on a daily basis. Look back at Part One, Chapter 1, for an example of a prioritizing method.

8. *Handle stuff once.*

Mail and other correspondence should be dealt with at once, not put off until later. Avoid repetition and strive toward completion of tasks the first time you attempt them. Break out of the habit of leaving things "half done." Train yourself to work toward completion and closure.

9. *Conquer procrastination.*

I saved this tip for last. Procrastination (the failure to make or carry out the arrangements to fulfill the goals you have set) is a problem that affects all but the most organized and dedicated student. Students can easily fall victim to the tendency to put off until tomorrow that which should be done today. A form of avoidance, procrastination may be a warning sign of some underlying fear, desire to avoid taking responsibility for one's life, or just plain laziness. The first step in combatting procrastination is to identify the cause of this draining and counterproductive behavior.

Fear of failure is often the root cause of procrastination. Students tend to avoid and put off working on what they don't feel they are good at. Any benefit or positive challenge presented by these avoided tasks is too easily lost by the fear of difficulty and potential negative outcomes.

Once procrastination begins, the student finds it even more difficult to break the avoidance cycle. The task grows in importance the more it is avoided, and one's ability to see the task clearly becomes muddled. Pretty soon the student can lose sight of the task altogether, and it becomes blown totally out of proportion—assuming the dimensions of a dinosaur instead of the mouse it really is. And we all know that dinosaurs must be avoided at all costs!

Procrastination can be conquered; these dinosaurs can be slain and made extinct. Utilizing the following six suggestions can enable you to gain control of your time and accomplish even the most dreaded tasks.

a. *Identify the fear and determine its causes.*

Are you putting things off because you are afraid of finding out that you can't do them, or that you won't be able to get the outcome you need, or that people won't like or accept you as a result? Identifying the fear is the first step in breaking the avoidance pattern. Common fears include: fear of failure, rejection, responsibility, lack of approval, loss of prestige or importance, and even fear of success. Can you identify one of these fears as the root of your procrastination? If so, ask yourself why it is important for you to be afraid of this outcome. What difference would it make really if this feared outcome were to occur? What is the probability that this feared outcome actually will occur? Often people develop irrational fears and unrealistic expectations of feared outcomes. If they can rationally analyze the situations, the need to avoid these anxiety-provoking situations is neutralized.

b. *Do a task analysis.*

People often lose their ability to see tasks clearly when they procrastinate. They tend to blow the tasks out of proportion and are unable to see what needs to be done to accomplish their objectives. A way to combat this problem is by doing a task analysis that reduces the task into smaller subtasks. Write down what it is you have been avoiding and then divide that into smaller, achievable subtasks.

It is very important at this stage to do something! The inactivity cycle must be broken—you must crawl before you walk. Start small; don't get discouraged by a long assignment. As any marathon runner will tell you, the finish line (26.2 miles down the road) is reached only by taking one stride at a time. Successful marathoners break the 26.2-mile race into smaller pieces (splits), set goals for these reduced segments and focus on attaining them in a manner that leads them across the finish line. Procrastination can be beaten in the same way.

c. *Weigh the consequences.*

Motivation to stop procrastinating can be developed either by focusing on the consequences of continuing avoidance or by beginning work. Which feels better to you? Which will lead to the desired outcomes?

d. *Create a deadline.*

Set a target date that is reasonable and attainable. In most cases the ultimate deadline for some assignment or task is determined by your professor. Work with this deadline, but also create subdeadlines along the way.

e. *Make a public commitment.*

Go public; tell someone of your intention to complete the task you've been putting off. Challenge that person to call your bluff and encourage her to check up on your follow-through. The fear of embarrassment from not carrying out your commitment may be enough to overcome the fear that initially triggered your procrastination.

f. *Reward yourself.*

Find ways to reward your efforts at overcoming your procrastination, no matter how small they are. If you have a difficult time coming up with potential rewards, look back to Part Two, Chapter 1. Learn to feel good about your successes and to minimize your setbacks.

With these nine general suggestions in mind, I would like to suggest a specific approach to scheduling and time management. This approach, which I call *The Deadline Schedule,* incorporates the concept of "due dates," academic and nonacademic needs, and flexibility. Figure 6 is an example of a deadline schedule that has been started for a ten-week term. As you can see, this scheduling method contains information essential for effective planning and management of learning activities within the framework of real-life requirements. This scheduling method can be supplemented by a daily schedule or priority "To Do" plan as long as it also is flexible.

The advantage of The Deadline Schedule is that it allows the student to see the term as a unified whole. It enables the student to anticipate impending work in advance. One can see the "big picture" and how the parts fit together to accomplish the long-term goal— successful academic performance. By organizing your term in this fashion, you will be better able to distribute and plan your work and extracurricular activities in an organized, noncrisis way. Of course, there is still no substitute for actually grinding out the work (the schedule won't do it for you), but at least you'll know what you have to do and when it must be done. You will be in control of your work and time rather than have your work control you. This, to me, is true academic freedom!

A blank deadline schedule form follows the partially completed example. Review this chapter and fill out this schedule for the time remaining in the term. I recommend that you carry this schedule with you wherever you go. Have it ready in case new requirements pop up. If they do, those can be added to your schedule before you have a chance to forget them or misplace the assignment.

It may also be a good idea to make a copy of this schedule and put it in a place where you can't avoid seeing it even if you want to. Tape it to your mirror or on your desk or bathroom door.

Review your schedule every day, preferably the first thing in the morning (even before brushing your teeth). Learn to anticipate what you have to do early in the day, thereby giving yourself maximum time to get it done.

SUNDAY	MONDAY	TUESDAY	WEDNESDAY	THURSDAY	FRIDAY	SATURDAY
		Registration 11:45 - 2:30	Classes Begin		Freshman Dance (Date ?) 9:00 -2:00	
Movie	Meet w/Psych Prof. to Discuss Assign. 3:15	Psych-Assign. #1 Due		Course Change Deadline	Quiz-Math	Football
Study All Day Movie	Library-Topic Search for History Paper Study Physics Study Psych	Topic Due—History Paper Study Physics	Study Math	Study Math Psych Test #1	Physics Lab #1 Due	Football
Go Home? (Eat & Sleep)	Physics Lab Quiz #1	Psych-Assign. #2 Due Work on Outline	Physics Test #1 Study Psych Work on Outline	Outline Due-History Paper	Quiz-Math	Study Physics Go Home?
Movie	Do Physics Lab	Study	STUDY! STUDY! STUDY!	Midterm Exam: History Psych-Test #2	Midterm Exam: Math Physics Lab #2 Due	Football-Homecoming Homecoming Dance
Finish Psych Assign. #3 Movie	Study	Psych-Assign. #3 Due Study	Physics Test #2	1st Draft History Paper Due Study Math	Quiz-Math	Parents Weekend Football
Parent Weekend Out for Dinner (Real Food!!) Study?	Study - AM? Physics Lab Quiz #2	Study	Study	Psych Test #3	Physics Lab #3 Due	Work on Psych Assign.
Type Paper Movie	Type	Psych Assign. #4 Due Type	Pre-Registration for Winter Term Study Math	History Paper Due Frat Bids Out Study Math	Quiz-Math	Football
			Study Finish Lab	Psych Test #4	Physics Lab #4 Due	STUDY!!!
STUDY!!!	Physics Lab Final		Physics-Final	History Final 10:00 - 12:00	Final Exam-Math 9:00-9:50 Leave for Vacation Bus-5:00 p.m.	CRASH!!

Figure 6. Deadline Schedule

SUNDAY	MONDAY	TUESDAY	WEDNESDAY	THURSDAY	FRIDAY	SATURDAY

Figure 7. Blank Deadline Schedule

Here are some *additional tips* to keep in mind when setting up a schedule.

- *The best time to review for a lecture course is right after the class meets.* Set aside 10-15 minutes after class to review your notes. Write in key phrases and content summary, and add to your notes by looking over the text and/or other students' notes. Get into the habit of hanging around after class with a few other students to discuss the class and compare notes.

- *The best time to review for a participation course (class discussion, seminar, etc.) is right before the class meets.* Spend 10-15 minutes before class meets to refresh your memory as to what is going to be presented. This form of anticipation will make the class more meaningful and the material presented easier to learn.

- *In general, study periods for one course should not be longer than two hours at a time.* Fatigue sets in rapidly, and most people begin to lose attention and concentration after a couple of hours. Take a break, do something different and not study-related for a few minutes, then get back to studying if you need to. Provide periodic "reward breaks" for successful studying. A candy bar, celery stick, cola, video game, or some other tangible reward lets you know you have accomplished something important and may provide motivation for future studying.

- *If possible, a quick exercise break or high-protein snack might be helpful to reduce your fatigue after prolonged study periods.* Exercise breaks reduce errors and improve performance and output in real-life work situations. You might achieve similar results with periodic exercise breaks when studying. A *warning* is necessary here, however: *Don't let your exercise break get so involved that you don't get back to studying.* Playing a full game of basketball or running a marathon is not exactly what I have in mind as an exercise break. I'm thinking more along the lines of a walk around the block or ten minutes on your stationary bicycle, a quick jog, or some aerobic exercises. Short, brisk walks increase feelings of energy (sometimes for several hours), can help make personal problems appear less serious, and can increase optimism.

- *Study periods for one course should be spaced out over the entire week, not concentrated on just one or two days.* Wednesday may be your regular laundry day, but it shouldn't be the only day you study chemistry. Small chunks spread over many days works better than one big chunk concentrated at one time. If possible, study each course daily. Even if you don't have an assignment in a course, get into the routine of reviewing your notes for that course every day.

- *When memorizing and learning details are required, study periods should be short and frequent.* Learn a few facts, take a break, memorize a few more, take another break, and so on. This process can minimize mental fatigue.

- *Study periods can be longer when learning general concepts and material where your mind can make connections with other concepts in a meaningful way.* You may be able to study the concept of photosynthesis or democracy for a longer period of time than when trying to memorize mathematical formulas.

- *Vary the order of the types of subjects studied.* Do not study subjects that are very similar (e.g., French and Spanish or Calculus I and Calculus II) one right after the other. Alternate courses studied so that they are dissimilar. In this way you may be able to avoid confusion and the interference of past learning on present learning. If you must study two or more similar courses in succession, schedule some form of activity between them to clear your mind; e.g., study Calculus I, then go for a walk, and then study Calculus II.

- *The most effective time for memorizing specific details and facts is right before you go to bed.* By doing this memorization just prior to going to sleep, you will be less likely to be distracted and confused with additional information, information that may interfere with your ability to store this less meaningful material in your memory bank.

Incorporating these tips into a flexible study schedule will allow for effective planning, organization and management of your time, the accomplishment of your goals, and academic success.

Chapter 3

INCREASE YOUR READING EFFECTIVENESS

Notes

It is estimated that the average college student reads more than 850,000 words a week when the preparation for a research paper and the reading of periodicals, such as newspapers and magazines are included. If read at a rate of 250 words per minute, this works out to around 57 hours each week, or about 8 hours per day of reading!

These numbers may be on the high side, but even if we take a conservative measure of four hours per day, when we consider the commitments students have in addition to reading, we can get a clearer picture of how important efficient, effective reading really is. The necessity for developing new strategic approaches seems apparent.

Few students develop and use strategic approaches to reading, however. The use of reading processes such as previewing and rereading written material is inconsistent and often ineffective. Improved reading strategies can be taught to students, and teaching students to use effective reading strategies is helpful in improving comprehension, vocabulary, and retention.

Reading is the cornerstone of most of your coursework. The method for increasing your reading effectiveness is one that I have developed myself. It is based upon the many foolproof study formulas that have been developed over the years that students have continually tried and successfully ignored. I have tried to factor in the essential elements of these many formulas and to present them in a simple, easily adaptable way. My acronym is ARAR—or, for the more technically minded students, $(AR)_2$—and it stands for "*Anticipate, Read, Act,* and *Review.*"

Anticipate

The first step for increasing your reading effectiveness is a sort of "preview of coming attractions." Before actually reading the material in front of you, prepare yourself by first skimming the pages. Your objective is to become familiar with what is to be read, to know in a general way what lies ahead. Just as you would look over a road map before driving to an unfamiliar destination, you would preview the material to be read to get any clues to what is to be learned and where you will end up. You might even want to recall what you already know about this material from past reading or study. Reading will be made easier if you are aware of what you are supposed to know before reading.

Learn to insert questions in the text while you preview. For example, turn chapter headings into questions as a way of guiding your attention on to subsequent passages. This process, called forward transfer, is a powerful way to improve reading effectiveness. Try to formulate questions that call for verbatim rote answers (e.g., definitions or calculations) as well as for conceptual understanding. The types of preview questions that you formulate depend upon the types of questions that will appear on your examinations; therefore, it is important to know this information beforehand. Ask your professor about his test format before reading the text and formulate your preview questions accordingly.

Anticipate the material to be read by:

- looking over chapter title(s)

- formulating questions

- looking at pictures, graphs, figures, etc., and reading captions

- noticing underlined or italicized words or formulas

- reading summary paragraphs or conclusions

- looking at study questions at ends of chapters

Read

The second step involves doing what you are supposed to do—read. *For long-term understanding of unfamiliar written material, reading must be comprehensive.* The reader must read most of the words in order to understand and comprehend. No great short cuts here; just do it. Don't be overly concerned with underlining or taking notes at this stage; just read and concentrate on what you are reading.

Reading effectively can be influenced by two factors over which you can exert some control. The first is attitude. *Developing a positive mental attitude toward reading will stimulate the reader to read more.* Try to develop an attitude of viewing reading as enjoyable, interesting, and profitable rather than as an activity that must be endured. A reader who is interested and involved will get more out of reading than one who views it as something simply to be gotten out of the way. One way to become more interested in your reading is for you to try to imagine yourself as part of what you are reading.

Relating a descriptive passage in the text to oneself in some way may improve memory and recall. This seems to be especially helpful in learning prose material. Referring material to oneself may be effective because it makes the items to be learned more meaningful or gets the learner more involved in the learning task. This may also facilitate memory by providing internal cues at the time of encoding and retrieval (more on memory in Part 2, Chapter 7).

When reading a passage, attempt to relate the material to your own real-life experiences. Note the similarities and differences between what you are reading and your own life. "Become" one of the characters in your novel or imagine yourself as part of the chemical formula or mathematical equation. By mentally engaging the reading material in this imaginary way, you may find your interest and reading enjoyment increased.

The second way in which you can influence your reading effectiveness is to learn new reading techniques. Speed-reading, phrase-reading, and survey-reading techniques are but a few of the many reading strategies developed by experts in improving reading performance. A detailed description of these approaches is beyond the scope of this book. Interested students may read K. P. Baldridge, *Seven Reading Strategies,* Greenwich, CT: Baldridge Reading Instruction Material (1979).

Act

The reader must do something with or to the ideas or concepts read if long-term comprehension is expected, and this action must occur quickly. Reading should not be just the process of covering the required number of pages in the shortest possible time. ("Phew, I got that finished—now what can I do next?!") Effective reading involves more than passing your eyes over the printed type. You need to do something immediately after reading to *encode* or *embed* the material into your memory bank. Successful reading (and studying in general) requires taking time to put things in your own words—immediately. Repeat—*immediately.*

The bulk of forgetting takes place within minutes after study, then tapers off gradually. Within 24 hours after reading, fifty percent or more of what is learned is forgotten—unless you do something with it that helps put it in your own words. Effective encoding apparently allows you to create meaningful memory patterns that last.

Possible actions you could take after reading include the following:

- Write down key terms, phrases, formulas, etc., in margins of texts, notebook, etc.

- Go back and underline or highlight key sections and words, etc.

- Answer study questions; do sample problems

- Quiz yourself verbally on content

- Get together with others in your class and ask each other questions on the reading

- Make topic/chapter headings into questions and answer them

- Make a simple outline of material read

- Coordinate material read with in-class notes

- Restate in your own words the essential definitions, ideas, formulas, concepts, and facts just read

- Use multiple senses (e.g., hearing, seeing, speaking, writing, acting out), which help in remembering. (See Figure 8.)

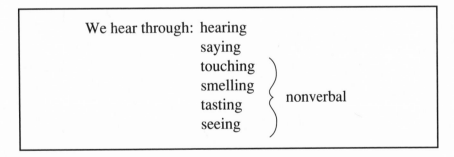

Figure 8. Reasons For Using Multiple Senses in Learning

Review

Material read should not be filed away and looked at again only when studying for a test. *Review and rereading increase comprehension and achievement.* The positive effects of review are even greater for students required to do so compared to students for whom review is optional. Therefore, if review is not required by your professor, make it a regular requirement yourself—force yourself to do this for every reading assignment undertaken.

Periodic review will keep things fresh and will retard spoilage (forgetting). *As you continue through the text, go back every so often and look at what you have already read.* Review your encoding activities; repeat some of your anticipatory behaviors; recall what you remember and add your new learnings to it. Don't let what you've read get away from you. This periodic review is a form of practice that will make future studying easier.

Chapter 4

TAKE EFFECTIVE NOTES

Education is a process whereby one person (a professor or teacher) attempts to impart knowledge to another person (a learner or student). A basic method used in this process is the lecture or class presentation, wherein the professor professes and the students record the words of wisdom. Students differ in their ability to take good notes. Many receive little or no instruction in this important activity.

Note-taking is a way of enhancing the storage of information in memory, thereby influencing both the quantity and quality of learning. Note-taking forces you to focus on and pay more attention to the material being presented. As a result you will tend to process the material presented more deeply and thereby learn it better. Taking notes has value because it increases attention during lectures and makes it more likely that the professor's ideas will be remembered.

Through the note-taking process you are guided to build mental connections between what is being presented in the lecture and what you already know. You are thereby encouraged (forced) to actively relate the new material to existing knowledge.

The chance of recalling a fact or information that is recorded in your notes is greater than for items not in your notes. There is no substitute for taking your own notes—not relying on a DN (Designated Note-taker). Students who take their own notes perform better on recall tests than do students who are just provided prepared lecture notes and those who take none at all.

In sum, note-taking effectiveness is positively related to learning outcomes in college lecture settings. Furthermore, effective note-taking can be strategically taught to students.

A warning on the use of your own lecture notes: Students' own notes generally tend to be incomplete and therefore are inadequate for effective studying and lecture review. Students who review their own notes and supplement these with teacher-prepared notes, notes from the text, and those of other classmates can overcome this problem.

My tips for improving your note-taking ability can be divided into four sections: anticipation skills; attending skills; actual physical note-writing skills; and skills designed to improve your note organization and review activities.

Anticipation Skills

The first step in effective note-taking is to get yourself primed and ready for the task at hand—taking good notes. This is similar to the first stage in the reading effectiveness plan previously discussed. The general goal here is to anticipate what the lecture/class presentation is going to be about—what are the topic and points to be presented?

Your ability to anticipate accurately varies with the topic and the professor. "Psych out" your professors. They are probably your most important learning resources. Learn to use those resources; understand their methods. You need to quickly learn the "style" of each. Does your professor stick closely to the course outline or text, allowing you to easily predict lecture content, or does she jump around randomly? Students who have taken courses with the professor in the past are good references; ask them. If the professor is new, probably in the first few classes you will get some clues about style; pay attention.

The course syllabus and assigned reading lists are two sources of cues about future lectures commonly available to students; use them to anticipate what the instructor will talk about on any given day. It is also important to listen carefully at the end of each class session. Amidst the noise of students closing their notebooks and gathering up their stuff for speedy exits, you may hear the teacher describing what will be covered during the next class. If you are still in the dark about what the next lecture is to cover, don't be afraid to ask the teacher. If nothing else, it will create the impression (true or not) that you care about what is being taught.

When you have a good idea of what the next lecture is going to cover, ask yourself these questions about your knowledge of the material:

Q - How much do I know about this topic already?

Q - How did the text, or other reading, cover this topic?

Q - How is this topic related to other parts of the course? to other courses?

Q - Based upon my knowledge of this instructor, what will be his orientation or bias toward this topic (excitement, boredom, pro-con)?

Attending Skills

Attending skills can be broken down into two subcategories: (1) *positioning* and (2) *listening*.

Positioning Skills

Where you sit in the classroom can influence your performance in the class. Many professors note a positive relationship between sitting toward the center of the classroom close to the front and receiving above-average grades. Their top students gravitate toward the seats best located for learning. This is, of course, impossible for everyone to do, but you could *make an extra effort to get to class early for the first week or so.* After that time everyone's "territory" is established, and seating positions remain fairly stable. (I doubt that seating position alone will guarantee As, but why not use all evidence to your advantage—every little bit helps!)

Picture a large, fat "T" running through the class as in Figure 9.

```
                              Professor

    X    •    •    •    •    •    •    •    •    X

    X    •    •    •    •    •    •    •    •    X

    X    •    •    •    •    •    •    •    •    X

    X    X    X    •    •    •    •    X    X    X

    X    X    X    •    •    •    •    X    X    X

    X    X    X    •    •    •    •    X    X    X

    X    X    X    X    X    X    X    X    X    X

    X    X    X    X    X    X    X    X    X    X

    X    X    X    X    X    X    X    X    X    X
```

Figure 9. The Success T

Try to *sit in a seat located within this "Success T."* Sitting in this area may prove advantageous to you because you will be:

- less distracted by other students and irrelevant stimuli

- in a good position to be recognized and to be able to ask questions

- less likely to talk, daydream, write notes

- better able to see the board and hear the instructor

- more in the instructor's "field of communication," allowing for more "personal/ intellectual contact" (may lead to subtle positive reactions toward you by the instructor)

- able to receive nonverbal communications more effectively

Listening Skills

Now that you are seated in the "proper" place and are in the "proper" state of preparation, readiness and attention, you will need to start listening in the "proper" way. Active and accurate listening is not easy and in many ways is much more difficult than reading. *Listening involves filtering out many stimuli, making value judgments as to what is important, and re-*

cording relevant remarks while remaining alert and continuing to listen. Pretty complex stuff when you think about it.

Your attending and listening ability can be improved if you:

- *Make a special effort to remember information presented around the middle of a lecture.* Items presented at the beginning and end of a series are those best remembered. Therefore, you need to stimulate yourself around the middle of a lecture when fatigue or boredom may momentarily set in. Try switching to a pen with different-color ink; do some isometric exercises; take a break to notice novel stimuli; yawn (physiological evidence indicates that yawning increases oxygen to the brain; but be careful—the professor may not know about this research!), or do some other activity to refocus your attention.

- *Become aware of emphatic cues during the lecture.* Each instructor has her own way to emphasize important content: voice inflection, pauses, repetition, verbal summary, writing on the board, handouts, etc. Attend to and analyze each instructor's lecture style and in-class behaviors as early in the term as possible.

- *Become an active, not passive, listener;* get involved and remember—learning is primarily your responsibility, not the professor's.

- *Listen with a purpose and with certain expectations in mind.* Learn to anticipate what the professor is going to lecture about. Prepare questions before the lecture and try to listen for the answers.

- *Make an immediate response to what is heard.* Don't wait before you record your notes. If you hear something that you think is important, write it down quickly.

- *Carefully observe the speaker.* Situate yourself within easy hearing and observing distance. Sit within the *"Success T"* whenever possible.

- *Attend to visual and environmental cues as well as verbal messages.* Learn to listen with your eyes as well as your ears.

- *Attend to and utilize silence.* Learn to use this time for thinking, analyzing and reviewing. Don't stop thinking when the professor stops talking.

- *Learn to filter out "noise."* Don't attend to conversations between other students or to other such distractions. If you are unable to do this successfully, assert yourself and ask for quiet or for help in quieting distractions.

Note-Writing Skills

Notes give visual emphasis to important ideas, facts, formulas, etc. Note-taking is a basic and critically important learning skill that could probably stand improvement. As I have mentioned, there is no substitute for active listening when taking notes. One must hear before one can record. Note-taking, like listening, is a complex, psychomotor skill. The following suggestions may improve your note-taking skills.

A. *Use abbreviations whenever possible.*

- It is possible to abbreviate frequently used words and still understand them. For example, *w* for *with* and *ch* for *chapter*. A statement such as *Rd ch 6 for next lect* is easily understood.

- Should an abbreviation be confusing, write out the word; e.g., does *no* mean *no* or *number;* does *wd* mean *word, wood* or *would*?

- *Go over your notes as soon as possible* after the lecture to clarify any confusing abbreviations, hard-to-read writing, or misunderstandings.

- Use plurals and other endings wherever appropriate; e.g., *rct, rctg, rctn* for *react, reacting, reaction.*

- Learn the standard abbreviations that have been developed in the field of study. They are usually available for frequently used words and phrases; e.g., $\longrightarrow$ signifies a chemical reaction and $\rightleftharpoons$ signifies a reversible chemical reaction.

- Abbreviations usually consist of the first letter and other significant letters of English words. There are exceptions of course; such as *e.g.* or *i.e.*, which originated in Latin.

- Vowels are the least noticed letters in the visual configuration of a word. Two types of most noticed letters are: ascenders and descenders—letters such as *t, h, l, g, y, q*, which extend either above or below the line; and letters at the beginnings or ends of words. Therefore, leave out vowels and middle letters when abbreviating.

- Some subject areas use Greek letters as symbols for operations or unknowns. Greek letters can be found in a dictionary under the heading "Alphabet," and this can be a useful resource for finding the meaning of this form of abbreviation.

- Here are some abbreviations that can be used in lecture notes. Can you add any? Are they confusing to you?

soln = solution	¶ = paragraph
w = with	ch = chapter
imp = important	th = theory
impr = improve	∴ = therefore
kn = know	prob = problem
kdge = knowledge	probs = problems
no. or # = number	mult = multiply
Δ = change	vol = volume
= = equals or equal	V = volume or velocity
≠ = unequal	> = greater than
abs = absolute	< = less than
sq rt or √ = square root	

B. *Date all notes and number all pages.* It is important to be able to quickly identify when your notes were recorded and where they fit into the chronological and topical flow of the lectures.

C. *Leave blank space on each page of notes for information missed.* Have plenty of room to add information missed during the lecture. The review process should stimulate you to clarify and add information. Don't worry about getting as many words as you can onto one page of notes. You should probably limit the amount of material on one page anyway to avoid confusion and "information overload."

D. *Develop a system to give extra emphasis to key ideas, concepts, definitions, etc.*

- underline
- use different-colored ink
- use asterisks
- draw arrows
- make flow charts or concept diagrams

E. *Coordinate your lecture notes with notes from the text.*

F. *Don't be overly concerned with neatness and style.*

Your lecture notes need be legible only to you. If you understand them, that's what counts. You don't need to impress your roommate with how nice your notes look as long as they help you learn. (The only exception to this principle is if your lecture notes are to be handed in and counted as a course requirement. In this case it is important for your professor to be able to understand what you have written.)

G. *Write more, not less.* Lecture notes containing more words are related to higher achievement than are notes with fewer words. Students frequently make the mistake of thinking (and probably have been told by unenlightened teachers) that notes should be brief and sketchy, but just the opposite may be true. Take comprehensive *and* complete notes.

H. *Give equal importance to all aspects of the lecture.* The professor's spoken words are just as important in helping you understand the lecture as is what is written on the board. Students tend to do a better job of recording information written on the board than of what the lecturer says. Don't ignore the importance of the professor's words just because they haven't been written out!

I. *Take notes during the entire lecture.* Students take almost 20 percent fewer notes in the second half of a lecture than in the first half. Keep with it and keep writing throughout the entire lecture.

Organizing and Reviewing Notes

Most students take notes in outline form. I think that this works because it allows you to get the main points of the lecture down and to avoid extra verbiage while maintaining some sense of organization and cohesion. I would like to suggest a modification of the basic outline method that may aid in retention and make future review and study easier: *The Key and Summary Method.* (See Figure 10.) This approach allows you to actively build connections between the material presented in the lecture and what you already know. Using summarization and paraphrasing, this method adds depth and breadth to lecture note-taking.

When taking your notes, leave rather wide margins on both the left and right sides of the page. The topic of the lecture should be written across the top of each page. The actual notes that you take during the lecture should be written down the center column. In the left- hand margin you should write key words representing each or every few lines of notes. The right margin should contain a one- or two-sentence summary of the page relating it to the topic of the lecture. The key words and summary statements should be written down during a review of your notes as soon as possible after class. (Remember, the typical student forgets about 50-60 percent of new material within 24 hours after it is presented.)

Key Words	**Date** **Topic Heading**	**Page #** **Summary**
Write Key words, formula name, date, concept, etc. ‾‾‾‾‾‾‾‾	Notes in outline form or form that works best for you. ‾‾‾‾‾‾‾‾‾‾ ‾‾‾‾‾‾‾‾‾‾	Summary of material in your own words, one or two sentences. ‾‾‾‾‾‾‾‾‾‾ ‾‾‾‾‾‾‾‾‾‾

Figure 10. The Key and Summary Method

KEY	DATE	NOTES	PAGE #	SUMMARY

The Key and Summary Method is helpful because it:

- helps you retain the lecture material by stimulating action and encoding

- encourages quick note review before too much is forgotten. (When scheduling your time it might be helpful to schedule 10-15 minutes right after class to review your notes and to write in key and summary statements.)

- forces you to think about the lecture material in terms of important, often interrelated, concepts rather than isolated facts

- helps build the vocabulary you will need for successful performance

- provides organized study material for tests

- saves future study time locating facts and filling in gaps in your lecture notes when the material is no longer fresh in your mind.

A variation of the Key and Summary Method can be used when you have reading assignments that cover the same topics discussed in a lecture. When taking class notes, use the Key and Summary Method on only one side of the opened notebook. Save the other side for notes from your readings. Record only those points from the reading that were not covered in the lecture. This variation is illustrated in Figure 11.

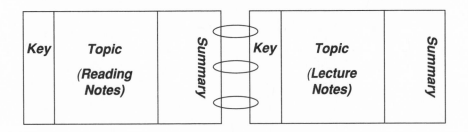

Figure 11. Variation of Key and Summary Method

Remember, effective note-taking involves anticipation of content, focused attention and active listening skills, appropriate manual note-taking abilities, and logical, easy-to-follow organizational structure. Review of your notes immediately after taking them will facilitate retention and retard forgetting.

A few words of warning are necessary at the end of this chapter. Implementation of these note-taking strategies cannot guarantee successful learning or high grades. Much still depends upon your professor and the degree of familiarity you have with the lecture material. Results seem best with professors who lecture at a moderately paced lecture rate and with moderately unfamiliar material. Note-taking strategies with professors who lecture very slowly or very rapidly and with material that is extremely unfamiliar or extremely familiar will not have as direct an impact upon future performance.

Regardless of this warning, learning effective note-taking skills will probably be helpful to most of you at some point in your academic careers. It is worth your time and energy to learn more effective note-taking strategies.

Chapter 5

CONTROL YOUR STUDY ENVIRONMENT

Your behavior is influenced by, among many things, your feelings, motivations, your history of rewards and reinforcements, and also by the immediate situation in which you find yourself. Your environment, all those things that surround you when you are studying, influences the quality and quantity of your efforts. Distracting stimuli, such as loud music, talking roommates, pictures of your girlfriend, or an opened bag of chocolate chip cookies, can interfere with your concentration and decrease your ability to study. Yet, students tend not to choose study environments that are free from distracting stimuli. (In fact, why don't you get up right now and turn off your stereo!)

Take a few moments to observe your present environment. Where are you sitting (or not sitting)? What does your desk look like? What sounds are floating through the airwaves? Are you alone? If not, what are the others doing?

Controlling your study environment to create conditions favorable to effective studying is an important, though frequently overlooked, dimension of study improvement. *THE BASIC RULE OF THUMB IS: Remove stimuli associated with nonstudy behaviors, those incompatible with your learning mission, and replace them with stimuli that will maximize your study frequency and effectiveness.* (In other words, clean up your room!)

Here are five specific suggestions to help you find and create a study environment that encourages studying:

1. *Don't study at a cluttered desk.* Remove all items not associated with the task at hand— studying. Extra books; papers; unanswered letters; food; pictures of friends, loved ones, family; and the like can serve only as distractions, causing your attention to wander and your concentration to be broken. Have only those materials necessary for your immediate studying (e.g., paper, pencil, text, notebook); clear your desk of everything else.

2. *Have as your "study place" a location (a kind of academic sanctuary) that is reserved for study and nothing else.* It makes no difference where this "study place" is; it could be in the library or in your room—or even in an empty classroom. What's important is to learn to associate this place with one, and only one, activity—studying. This will help you to focus your attention. You may also find that you are able to decrease the time it takes to warm up to your subject because you will automatically be in the right frame of mind for studying when you come to your "study place." You will come to associate this place with studying and will not have to combat associations with nonstudying that other places in your room, dorm, or library may have. Studying while lying on your bed or while in the TV lounge or the periodical section of the library may tempt you to think about (or do) things that will not help your study efforts.

3. *The probability of studying occurring is increased not only if it is practiced under the same conditions but also at the same time each day.* Studying at the same place at the same time with the same learning materials each day may increase the frequency and, therefore, the effectiveness of studying. Establish a study routine, and after a while it will seem natural to study under those conditions. You may even notice that not studying causes you to experience some mild anxiety, discomfort, and guilt.

4. *Post your goals/objectives near your desk.* At the beginning of each term make a list of the specific goals or objectives that you will attempt to achieve during this time. Having them visible when you study may serve to focus your attention on studying in order to reach these targets.

5. *Have your deadline schedule handy and refer to it before and after each study session.* Learn to anticipate and prioritize, and redo the schedule daily. Make your schedule become part of your everyday study environment.

Take a few moments at this time to describe your typical study environment. What does it look, sound, feel like?

_____

_____

_____

_____

What can you do to improve this situation in order to reduce distraction and maximize concentration?

_____

_____

_____

_____

Where else on campus could you study, if you chose, that would present an environment most conducive to studying?

_____

_____

_____

_____

Chapter 6

IMPROVE YOUR CONCENTRATION

Attention is a necessary prerequisite for learning. *Concentration means focusing your full attention on the task at hand.* What makes concentration so difficult, however, is that our environment usually provides us with more information than we can handle at one time. Our senses are constantly bombarded with stimulation, most of which is either insignificant or extraneous to our study efforts or repetitive. Selective, focused attention is the ability to attend to one aspect of a stimulus or range of stimuli while ignoring the irrelevant parts. This filtering and focusing of attention is what I mean by concentration.

One's ability to concentrate is also somewhat dependent upon the ability to discriminate between competing stimuli. For example, reading effectiveness is enhanced if you can distinguish between, and therefore attend to, the written words in the text instead of the words that your favorite rock group is singing on the stereo. If you can learn to filter out your thoughts (which can be considered to be internal verbalizations) concerning your hot date for this coming weekend and maintain your focused attention on the material you are studying, you are concentrating effectively. *Concentration, then, is your ability to maintain focused attention, to discriminate between appropiate and inappropriate stimuli, and to avoid distracting thoughts.*

Concentration is made all the more difficult because different stimuli have different relevance or importance for each individual, and this relevance can shift rapidly. If thinking about your date is more important than studying, it will be difficult for you to study. Your concentration will be disturbed because of this competition for your attention. This dilemma can be resolved if you do one or both of two things: motivate yourself to increase the importance of studying over fantasizing about your date and/or stop studying and focus all your attention on the distracting or irrelevant stimulus, your date in this example.

For many people, studying is not the most pleasant or self-rewarding task. Therefore, distractions are probably difficult to avoid, and divided attention is a pretty common occurrence. People fall victim to a "mind" that wanders instead of staying focused on the task at hand. This is not helpful when trying to study. You've probably been a victim of poor concentration and divided attention if after a few pages of reading you find yourself unable to remember what you have just read.

The study of perception provides another avenue for us to understand the effects of interfering thoughts upon concentration. Perception is the process of becoming aware of one's environment by way of the sense organs. Sensory content, such as sounds, sights, smells, is always present in our realm of conscious awareness. What is actually perceived is often the product of several factors: past experiences, how the sensory stimuli are organized, one's learned pattern of response tendencies (called "psychological set"), and the human need to get closure on incomplete stimuli.

The need for closure is of special interest to our discussion of perception and how it relates to attention, concentration, study skills, and academic success.

Humans, it seems, have a tendency to "fill in the gaps" when stimulation is incomplete. We seem to want to get completion on stimuli that are incomplete and that make sense only as completed wholes. For example, look at the the following two figures. What do you see?

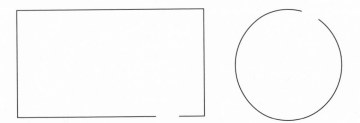

Figure 12. Illustration of Closure Phenomenon

Your first reaction may have been to perceive the two figures as a rectangle and a circle—incomplete but still obviously a rectangle and a circle. Did you perceive them as two oddly shaped lines? In fact, this is just what they are. Our minds have the tendencies to complete incomplete stimuli for us, which has advantages (such as in problem solving), but which is disadvantageous when it comes to concentration.

One such disadvantage of this mental tendency for closure is the recurrence of incomplete thoughts, or "unfinished business," into conscious awareness. These thoughts may prove distracting and break our concentration as they keep popping into our minds when trying to read or study!

As a way of understanding this tendency for closure better, let me use what I call the "Beach Ball Metaphor." Figure 13 illustrates this.

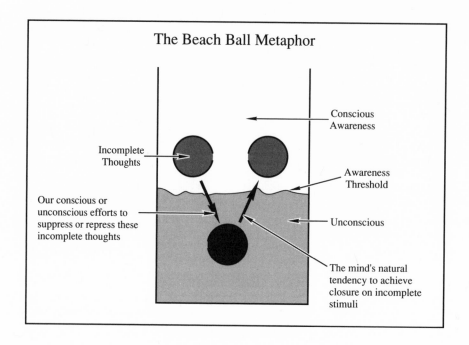

Figure 13. The Beach Ball Metaphor

The beach ball represents a nagging, incomplete thought or some type of unfinished business represented by an internal mental statement, such as "I should really call my girlfriend," or "What am I going to do this weekend?" or "I should be studying math now instead of history." This thought is distracting to our concentration, so we try to forget it by "pushing it out of our minds."

We may consciously or unconsciously try to push this thought below the level of conscious awareness, hoping it will go away and let us get on with our studying ("out of sight, out of mind"). However, the mind's tendency to get closure on incomplete stimuli counteracts these avoidance or defense efforts and forces the beach ball (incomplete thoughts) back to the surface into consciousness and into our perceptual field again. Often the force of the beach ball crashing out of the water creates a larger splash and distraction than did our efforts in pushing it down in the first place. Our concentration once again is broken. This pattern will probably continue as long as we attempt to ignore or suppress the nagging incompleted thought.

Another way of removing the beach ball from the pool (awareness) involves a more direct and active approach. Instead of pushing it below the surface of the water, we simply could pick it up, handle it properly and place it outside of the swimming pool altogether. In other words, *if we attend to the interfering thought directly and act in such a way as to finish or complete the thought, it will dissipate and cease to be a distraction.* Closure is attained, the mind is satisfied, and focused concentration can again be attained.

I call an approach to improving concentration based upon this metaphor the *Closure Technique*. This technique is derived from an approach suggested by Newman, Sansbury, and Johnson (1976) at American University. The object of this approach is the neutralization of interfering thoughts by attending to them and setting aside time to think them out or resolve them through timely action. There are seven steps to the Closure Technique.

Step 1. This involves the accurate recording of your study efforts. Across the top of a piece of paper write:

Date   **Time Begun/Ended**   **Thoughts**   **Elapsed Time**

Step 2. Write the date and time begun and then begin studying, reading, or other learning activity you are engaged in.

Step 3. When you become aware of a thought that interferes or competes with your concentration, make a slash (/) under the "Thoughts" column. Then quickly try to return to your work.

Step 4. Continue this study/recording process until you have made five (5) slashes. This indicates that these interfering thoughts are of some importance to you and probably should be dealt with in order for you to be able to concentrate fully.

Step 5. After the fifth slash is recorded, mark down the time in the "Time Ended" column, calculate the elapsed time since you began studying and enter that in the column so labeled.

Step 6. Put the material aside, leave the immediate study area and act upon your distracting thought(s) in a way that will lead to resolution and closure. How you act can vary. It might be sufficient to close your eyes and spend a few moments thinking the thought(s) through. Or it might require a telephone call home to inform your parents when to expect you for the coming holiday vacation. If a decision can be made concerning any of these interfering thoughts, make it; act upon it immediately. If you decide nothing can be done at this time, accept the reality of that conclusion. Tell yourself something such as "I can't do anything about that now, so I will focus on that which I can control and go back to studying." Settle what's on your mind, focus your attention on the interference and diffuse it (remove it from the pool!)

Step 7. When you feel comfortable with your resolution(s) of the interference, go back to studying. Begin again by recording the time begun studying on the next line in the appropriate column. Record each interfering thought as before until you have five, then proceed as above.

Initially your goal should be 30 minutes of good studying (excluding the time when you are resolving your interfering thoughts). You can expand the "good studying" time until you can accomplish the two-hour time period previously suggested. At first you may find that it can take up to one hour to meet your goal of 30 minutes. As you progress you'll find that you have fewer interferences and more good study sessions.

A few words of caution—it may be easy to abuse this technique and use it as a way of avoiding your work altogether. Don't spend an inordinate amount of time resolving your interfering thought(s). Remember, your goal at this time is to improve the quality and quantity of your studying, *not* to resolve all of life's problems. Attend to the distractions that realistically can be dealt with quickly without requiring that you completely remove yourself from your study environment.

Chapter 7

IMPROVE YOUR MEMORY SKILLS

Notes

This chapter is about how human memory works and how you can improve it. The goal of the chapter is twofold. First, I would like to introduce you to some information about the process by which people learn, memorize, and remember. I will describe an information-processing model that explains how people transform, store, recover, and use information. Second, I will discuss some practical memory aids you can use to improve the quantity and quality of what you remember.

If you are able to understand how memory works in a general, abstract way—if you can mentally visualize a model of memory—then your ability to remember seems to be improved. Knowledge about learning, about the mechanisms involved in memory, enables students to understand the process and to study more effectively.

Computer models are helpful in understanding memory and can enhance learning. An "information-processing" model of human learning, similar to that of a computer, can be useful in conceptualizing how memory works. This model is presented in Figure 14; it shows the processes by which humans attend to, encode, store, act upon, and retrieve information.

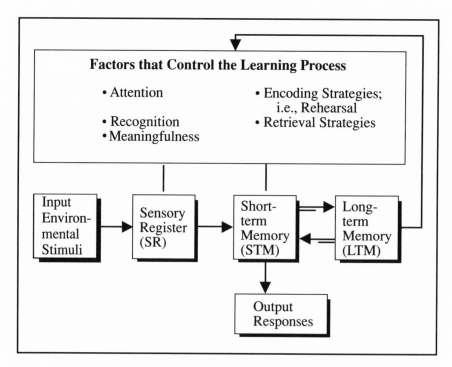

Figure 14. Information-Processing Model of Learning

This model identifies the memory storage areas and what controls the learning process. The memory storage areas vary in the quantity of information that actually can be stored. The control processes influence the flow of information between memory storage areas and how that information is stored. An important element in this model is the role that you, the learner, play in the learning process. You as the learner are in control of the information-processing process in that you decide how and when to employ the control processes. *The control processes—recognition, attention, rehearsal, and retrieval—are influenced by your direct, conscious manipulation.*

"Fred The Head" (Figure 15) illustrates this information-processing model in more "human" terms and may help you to better understand this concept.

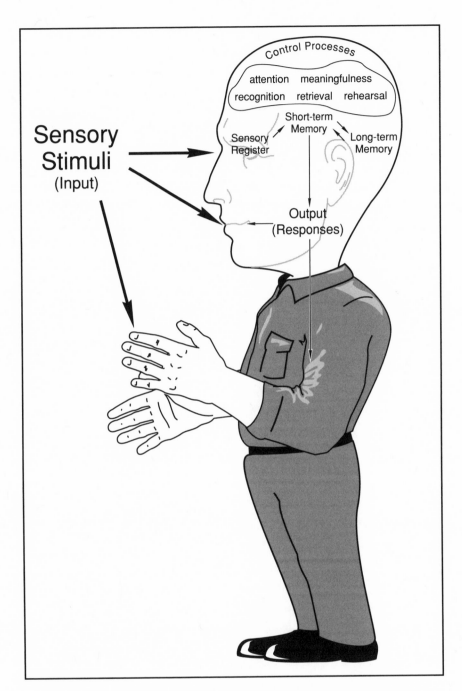

Figure 15. "Fred the Head"—An Information-Processing Model of Memory Comes Alive!

The Sensory Register (SR) is the beginning point of information processing and has environmental stimuli as its basis. The SR acts to process and filter the numerous sights, sounds, smells, tastes, and physical sensations that constantly bombard your sense organs. The purpose of the SR is to hold information just long enough (one to three seconds) for you to judge whether or not you should attend to it further. The SR has a limited capacity of about 12 pieces of information. Control processes that determine whether or not information stored in the SR will progress to more long-lasting memory stores are recognition and attention. *Information that is noticed and is recognizable because of experience will be more easily processed and remembered.*

When information has been attended to and recognized as meaningful, it can be moved into Short-Term Memory (STM). *Learning is made easier when the material to be learned is meaningful—when you know something about the material—as opposed to material that is new to you.* Short-Term Memory, often referred to as "working" memory since you are actively involved with this information at the moment, is a place where information is held for only 20 seconds or so. Not only is Short-Term Memory brief, it is limited to approximately seven unrelated chunks of information at a time.

Information quickly disappears from STM unless it can be rehearsed. Rehearsal corresponds to the *Active* learning component described in the General Formula for Academic Success in Part One, Chapter 7. Rehearsal can serve to hold information in STM for immediate use or can help to move information to long-term memory stores.

The third memory storehouse, Long-Term Memory (LTM), is unlimited in its storage capacity and may be permanent. In fact, your LTM may permanently store everything you have ever learned. (A little scary, isn't it!) If this is true, forgetting may not be a memory storage or memory decay problem but a retrieval problem, an inability to unlock and decode what you have learned and stored in LTM.

Information is stored in LTM through a process of encoding that builds upon the organization and meaningfulness of the items you are trying to learn. *Well-organized material and information that is meaningful, which "connects" with prior learning, will be learned more quickly, encoded into LTM, and retained for future retrieval.* In other words, the likelihood of remembering something depends directly upon the quality of your encoding activities.

The control processes proposed by this information-processing model are the elements that you directly influence; they therefore deserve further elaboration.

Attention, as discussed previously in the chapter on concentration, is a focusing process that enables you to select the appropriate stimuli for further mental activity. You can arrange or modify stimuli to enhance their attention-getting characteristics and thus aid in the learning process.

Qualities such as the size, intensity, color, unexpectedness, or novelty of a stimulus influence your tendency to attend to it. Make your lecture notes stand out by alternating ink color, the size of key words, the spacing and margins. If there is some item of information that is vital to learn, try something that will grab your attention, such as turning your paper upside down and taking notes. This certainly will make an impression when you study this information later in the term.

Recognition relates to your ability to notice the sensory stimuli presented and to relate them to information previously stored. When studying, attempt to recognize key words, diagrams, and concepts and connect them in a meaningful way to what you already know.

Rehearsal, repetition, and practice are essential for encoding material into short-term and long-term memory. The Action element in the General Formula for Academic Success emphasizes this. To maintain previously learned material and to learn new material will require more than one reading of your notes or text. Studying is just another term to describe Rehearsal, Repetition, and Practice.

The *organization of material to be learned can be a powerful aid in learning. Your ability to group information together, thereby creating meaningful structure and reducing the number of bits of information, makes learning easier.* Well organized notes, for example, may lead to more efficient learning because there are fewer chunks of information to learn and because each new fact may serve as a cue for the one that follows.

Your ability to relate new learning to that which has previously been learned will also enhance the learning process. This ability to make learning meaningful will facilitate encoding of information into LTM because the new material will be more easily associated with familiar memories and previously stored knowledge.

Visual Memory Procedures

The use of mental pictures or visual images of information is helpful for encoding material into LTM. Concrete material that can be seen in your "mind's eye" is more easily remembered than abstract material. Retrieval is made easier because there are more potential cues to unlock or decode the material from LTM. Learning the word "horse" is easier than learning the word "noun" because you can visualize a mental picture of a horse and associate it with something that has real meaning for you. *I encourage you to try forming a mental image of what you are trying to learn—see it, hear it in your mind in addition to saying it out loud.* Utilize as many ways as possible to encode the material into LTM.

Take a few moments at this time to construct a mental picture of some concept, fact, or procedure that you are currently studying. For example, reconstruct the information-processing model presented in Figure 14. Close your eyes and see each memory storage area in your mind's eye; follow the control process arrows. Now repeat this visualization procedure for material from one of your courses.

Mental visualization or directed imagery can be a very helpful way of acquiring a skill and improving performance. Picture yourself calm, relaxed, confident, and knowledgeable in a testing situation and you may be able to "trick" your body into reacting in that way when actually taking the test.

Using Learning Strategies as Memory Aids: Concept Mapping, Category Clustering, and Networking Techniques

An interesting extension of the use of imagery to improve memory involves the application of graphic aids or diagrams to reinforce in-depth encoding of new information. Building upon the essential memory principles of meaningfulness and organization, learning strategies such as concept mapping, category clustering, and the network technique have been developed.

A learning strategy is an integrated series of information-processing behaviors that are used for learning and remembering. In simpler terms, it is a study technique that enables you to see the subject matter more clearly.

Learning strategies are systematic, integrated techniques that clearly illustrate what is being learned and how specific pieces of information are interrelated.

Category clustering and *concept mapping* are types of verbal encoding procedures that may be helpful when trying to learn lists of formulas, facts, or other such information. Placing objects into categories based upon some common characteristic aids in learning. Creating hierarchies can also be a helpful learning tool. *Organization facilitates memory.* Figures 16 and 17 present two examples of this form of visual encoding procedure.

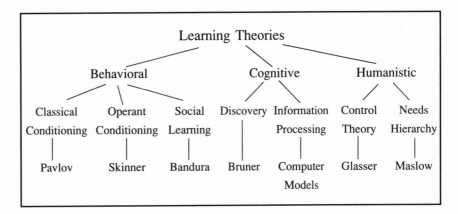

Figure 16. Concept Mapping

This type of illustration visually presents important concepts or facts and shows the relationships among them. This technique *allows you to see the subject matter more clearly, making the separate pieces of information more meaningful and thereby easier to learn.*

The network technique is another type of graphic learning strategy. It was designed to help students organize, integrate, and elaborate on reading assignments but can be used for those same purposes when studying lecture notes.

The objective of networking is to identify concepts and principles and to illustrate their interrelationship in terms of networks. The contents of these diagrams are short summaries of what is to be learned. The relationships can take the form of hierarchies, chains, and/or clusters. The result is some form of diagram or other visual representation of the information, with each piece connected to the others in an appropriate way. Figure 18 illustrates an example of the network technique.

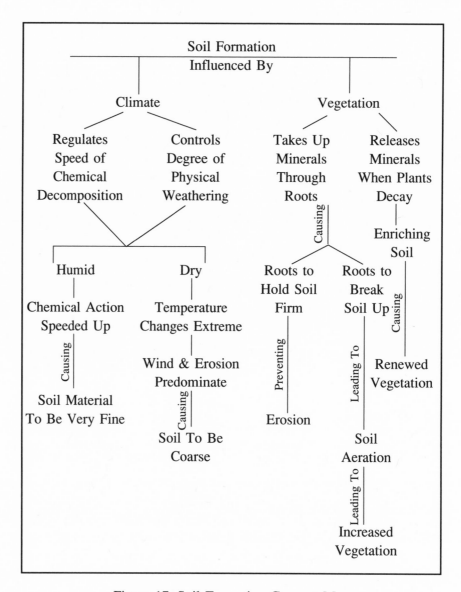

Figure 17. Soil Formation Concept Map

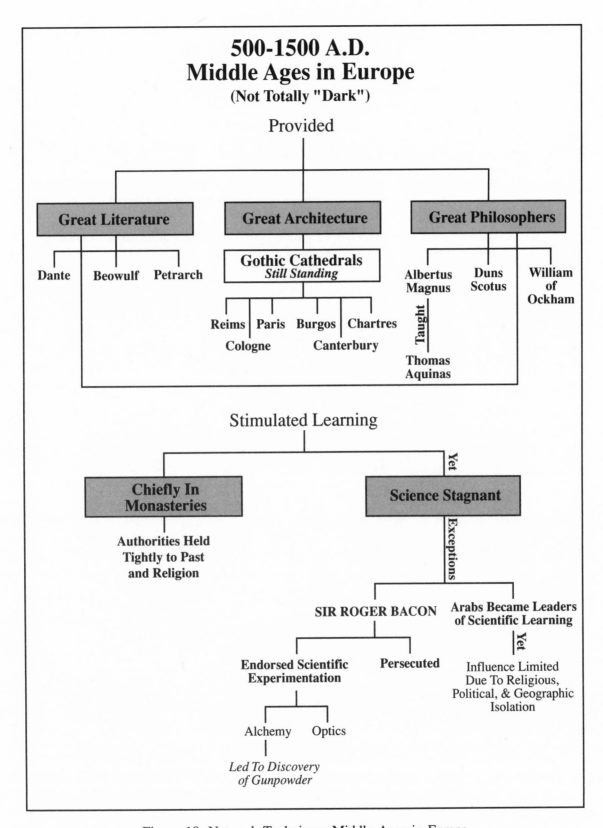

Figure 18. Network Technique: Middle Ages in Europe

The preceding discussion of memory and the use of learning strategies can be seen as an attempt to improve your learning and knowledge through an understanding of how your learning and memory work and the application of this knowledge to your actual study behaviors. The term used to describe this process is *Metamemory,* or *Metacognition,* and *means the application of knowledge of how we think and learn to the improvement of learning.* The knowledge that interesting material is remembered better than noninteresting material; or that larger amounts of material take longer to learn than smaller chunks; or that the longer one waits between learning and recall, the more one is liable to forget are all examples of metamemory. *Knowing about the process of learning will make learning easier and more effective.* College students have the mental ability to understand and apply this principle of learning—and in a sense this is the bottom-line goal of this entire book. Learning how to learn works! It makes preparation for exams easier and improves your memory and academic performance.

The following pages of this section on memory will focus on some additional techniques, called mnemonic devices, that can be used to improve recall of important information. These strategies also try to capitalize on making the material to be learned more meaningful or better organized.

Mnemonic Devices

Most students are rather inefficient learners. This may be true whether you get good grades or poor grades. Attempts at encoding information into LTM rarely go beyond simple rote rehearsal, such as reading and rereading a text or lecture notes, outlining or underlining. Most students' memory potentials go unutilized or underutilized, and rarely are they taught techniques to expand these potentials. Yet, many memory aids are readily available to students, and some of these have been around for centuries. These memory aids—called *mnemonic devices*—vary in their ease of application, but the effort can result in improved memory, comprehension, and academic performance.

Mnemonic devices are simply systematic learning procedures that help organize and store information and improve memory. Their effectiveness rests upon the principles of organization and meaningfulness, making use of visual and verbal imagery and category clustering.

Mnemonic devices may seem to be overly complicated procedures, but regular, naturally occurring learning processes are also very complex in their use and development; you just don't attend to them in systematic ways. Don't dismiss the mnemonic devices as too complex before you try them.

Individual and cultural factors may influence your ability to learn and utilize mnemonic memory aids effectively. Keep this in mind if you decide to try to learn a mnemonic device, and don't get overly frustrated if you experience some difficulty.

Here are some examples of mnemonic devices. Try them out; see how they work for you.

A. *Rhyme Mnemonic.* A very simple approach of making a rhyme with the material to be learned. Most school-children learn "i before e except after c" or "Thirty days hath September, April, June, and November." These are classic examples of rhyme mnemonics.

B. *Acrostic.* Similar to an acronym except letters are used to form a sentence. Make up a sentence using the first letter of each word of the material to be learned. For example, *"Every Good Boy Does Fine"* is an acrostic used to remember the names of the five lines of a music staff.

C. *Pegword.* This mnemonic is useful in learning lists of information. The idea here is to use words as pegs upon which to hook, or tie, items to be learned. You try to associate a visual image of the to-be-learned item hooked to the peg. One frequently used set of pegwords that are easily visualized is: one-bun, two-shoe, three-tree, four-door, five-hive, six-sticks, seven-heaven, eight-gate, nine-mine, ten-hen. The words "bun," "shoe," "tree," etc., form pegs that stand for the numbers. A list of items up to ten can be remembered using these pegwords by hanging each to-be-learned item to a peg. For example, if you needed to remember a list of items to be bought at the school bookstore you could associate each with a pegword; e.g., a pencil sticking in a bun, a ruler stuck in a shoe, notebook paper wrapped around a tree, and so on.

D. *Loci or Place Strategy.* This method has been used since ancient Grecian times and works very well for recalling large amounts of information. The first step in using the loci method is for you to memorize some mental pictures of a series of familiar places. Commonly used loci are rooms in your house, buildings on campus, and stores on a street. The loci should be close together so they form a natural series. You should develop a large number of places, with 10 to 12 as a minimum. Number the loci in the series starting with one and proceeding to the end of your list. Make sure you select places that are highly familiar to you. Vary the appearance of the loci to reduce confusion and emphasize the distinctive features of each. You can expand the number of loci by picturing a few key elements within each place. For example, if you select the rooms of your house as your loci, picture a few pieces of furniture within each room. You then can use these pieces of furniture to help you remember even more information.

After you have selected your loci, form images of the items you want to remember and place each image in a locus as you mentally walk from one place to another. When you want to recall the stored information, simply retrace your steps through each locus, retrieve the item, and decode it into the appropriate spoken or written form.

E. *Key-Word Method.* This memory technique has been shown to be effective in learning vocabulary and foreign languages. The key-word mnemonic technique involves the three essential components of all associative learning devices—*recoding, relating,* and *retrieving.* For example, an unfamiliar word, such as *dahlia* (a flower), is recoded into a more familiar word, *doll.* This is the key word and it has the added helpful property of sounding similar to the word to be learned, *dahlia.* The next step in learning is to semantically relate the key word to the vocabulary word's meaning. For example, picture a doll sniffing a flower. Later, the meaning of *dahlia* can be systematically retrieved by retracing the path from *dahlia* to *doll* to a *doll sniffing flowers* to *flower.*

In summary, mnemonic devices and learning strategies can be easy to learn and are interesting methods for improving one's memory. Motivation to learn, as well as self-control for learning, can be simultaneously stimulated through utilization of these memory aids.

Chapter 8

PLAY (AND WIN) THE TEST "GAME"

Notes

Your college education is a cumulative experience made up of a series of different courses taught by a series of different instructors. Ideally, your attention is focused in one area of study, your major, but you are required to take courses in other disciplines as well.

The teaching and learning process as practiced in college requires that you see each particular subject through the eyes of each individual professor. Your job is to integrate, in direct or indirect ways, these different perspectives into your own unified system of knowledge, learning, and "truth." What each course is about, and what you are tested and graded upon, is your ability to view the material from your professor's individual perspective.

In some respects, testing and grading can be viewed as a "game" of being able to learn and understand the instructor's "truth"—his personal and somewhat subjective version of the important facts, concepts, and interpretations that make up the subject being taught. This is a serious "game," with a high entry fee (called tuition), played for high stakes—with critical and far-reaching consequences. Conditioning yourself for the "game" makes sense, and learning the rules and regulations is essential. One of the most basic rules of the college "game" is that there needs to be a way to measure and assess learning and performance. A fact of college life is that grades must be assigned (even if they are called Pass/Fail), and exams and tests are the most common way this is done. *Winning at college can boil down to being able to succeed at taking exams, being able to play and win the successive series of testing "games" set out before you.*

It is important to realize that, unlike people, all tests are not created equal! I have attempted to identify the most common testing procedures and to provide some suggestions as to how you can best score at each differing "game." However, before looking at specific strategies for specific tests I would like to offer a few general suggestions that may be helpful in maximizing success in all test-taking situations.

General Test-Taking Strategies

1. *Prepare yourself mentally and emotionally by viewing a test as a challenge or opportunity to perform, not as a punishment.* Students typically view testing as the way instructors monitor and assign measures (grades) of how much the students know about particular topics. Tests are usually seen in a negative light. You can learn to reverse this, however, by viewing testing as a real, tangible motivation factor leading to more effective studying.

   Tests, especially those given during the term, can be viewed as learning opportunities to prepare you for future exams. *Tests create a heightening and focusing of attention, help to cue you in on relevant information, and provide experience with test format and questioning style.* Each of these functions of tests can contribute to future learning and retention of studied material.

   The value of viewing tests as learning opportunities is heightened in courses where there are cumulative final examinations covering the entire content of the course from term beginning to end. In those situations tell yourself that you are beginning the study process for the final when you start to prepare for the first in-term exam. Self-prepared study exams may also be very helpful, and I encourage you to try to write and answer your own exams as a general study aid.

   I can't overestimate the importance of approaching each test with a *positive mental attitude* and an expectation of success. An application of a basic law of psychology states: *Students who expect tests to be negative ordeals and those who view tests as positive opportunities to "strut their stuff" usually get what they are looking for!* It is critical to be able to "psych" yourself up to a point of expecting to do well (backed up, of course, by adequate preparation and studying).

   The correlation between positive expectation and grades on university exams has been demonstrated in many studies. Positive expectations measured shortly before an exam have also been shown to be good predictors of persistence of effort during the exam itself. Expecting success seems to have motivational consequences in the testing situation and thereby helps determine positive performance outcome. Students who expect to do well on tests seem to try harder during the test and get rewarded for their efforts.

Take a few moments before every exam and sit quietly, reflecting on the fact that you expect to do well. Tell yourself that you know the material and you *will* demonstrate this knowledge on the test.

2. *Learn to anticipate what is going to be on the exam.* One way to do this is to identify the perspective and orientation of the professor. Early in the term begin to discover the key issues and individual teaching and evaluation approaches of each professor. Get as much information as you can about her past tests, grading procedures, and course-material weighting priorities; i.e., how much emphasis is put on the different parts of the subject matter. Review what I have written previously about anticipation in Part Two, Chapter 4 on note-taking and in Part Two, Chapter 3 on reading effectiveness.

3. *Begin your test preparation activities as far in advance as you can.* Effective studying for tests means planning ahead and effectively managing time. *Don't cram if you can avoid it.* By cramming I mean a last-minute, last-ditch effort to learn new material. Cramming is different from last-minute review to summarize or brush up on previously learned information.

4. *Practice. Repetition and small chunks of information are key concepts for test taking.* Just as an athletic team practices plays over and over until they become almost automatic, you should strive to break your studying into small units and practice, practice, practice. Construct a mock test and answer your own questions.

5. *Study with others if you can.* Study groups assist students with the synthesis of course material and generate energy and commitment (i.e., motivation) among the group members.

Studying in pairs or in groups can be more effective than studying individually. Cooperative learning seems to lead to positive outcomes when learning technical, procedural material as well as fact-based, nontechnical information.

As a member of a study group, you become both learner and teacher, increasing your comprehension of important material. Each study group member becomes an active learner, which leads to becoming a better learner. An additional advantage of studying with others is that it widens your perspectives; it allows for the infusion of different views, different "truths," as group members share their ideas and opinions. Exposure to the thinking of others may enable you to break out of the confinement of one "mind set" or perception of "truth." This is especially helpful if your view is wrong or overly complicated or if the test asks you to present different arguments or solutions to a problem.

Study groups should be formed early in the term. You can do this by asking friends who share the class with you or those who sit nearby to join. Post a "Study Group Sign-Up Sheet" in your classroom or ask the professor to recruit study partners by announcing your intention to form a study group.

Things your study group can do to facilitate learning include: making up mock questions or practice tests; reviewing lecture and reading notes together; verbally quizzing each other; debating the pros and cons of key issues; taking turns playing the role of professor and teaching the other group members; brainstorming what you think will be on the exam; dividing up homework questions; and comparing homework answers.

6. *Be there and be ready.* At test time your task is simple—to demonstrate what you know. There is no need at this time for further learning. That task should have been accomplished during your pretest study and review. I do not recommend last-second cramming, asking of or answering questions from other students, reading, or review. *Get to the class early enough to get seated, settled and relaxed—but not so early that you get caught up in the last-minute study panic that often occurs.* Five to ten minutes before the scheduled starting time for the test is soon enough. Bring only the materials necessary for performing on the exam (e.g., paper, pencil, pen, calculator, watch, ruler, eraser, etc.,); leave all unnecessary texts or notebooks at home.

I would also recommend that immediately before you arrive at your testing room you reward yourself with some pleasurable, relaxing activity. Go for a quiet walk, listen to a relaxing record, play your guitar, take a soothing shower or bath, have an ice cream cone. Do something that communicates to you that you're prepared, you've done the best you can, and that things will work out fine. Once again, your pretest goal is positive mental attitude.

7. If you notice nervousness during the exam, learn to relax and control test anxiety. Chapter 9, Manage Test Anxiety, is devoted to an in-depth analysis of test anxiety and presents suggestions about how to control and reduce nervousness.

8. Read all directions before you begin the test—obvious, but often ignored. Figure 19 illustrates the importance of following directions. Take a few minutes to complete this exercise.

(Directions can seem quite complex when, in fact, careful reading can make them simple and clearcut. Follow these directions and see how you do.)

a. Read over everything before doing anything, but work as quickly as you can.

b. Write your name on the upper right hand corner of this page.

c. Circle the word "name" in the sentence immediately preceding this one.

d. Draw an "X" in the lower left-hand corner of this page.

e. Count out loud in your normal speaking voice backwards from ten to one.

f. Write the name of your academic major in the following space.

———————————————————————————————

g. Now that you have read the directions carefully, do only what sentences one and two ask you to do.

h. Don't give this activity away by any comment or explanation. Try it out on a friend.

Figure 19. How to Follow Directions: A Work Sheet to Improve Your Personal Skills

Don't be too anxious to get started. Make sure you fully understand the rules before you start the game. After writing your name in the appropriate place, put your pen or pencil down and carefully read the directions or test instructions.

9. *Look over the entire examination before answering any questions.* Notice whether the directions are the same for all parts of the test or whether you have a choice of questions to answer. Preview the exam just as recommended in the $(AR)_2$ method discussed previously.

10. *Read the test questions carefully.* Put your pen or pencil down when you read as a safeguard against answering too quickly. When you

understand what is being asked, you then can begin to think of the best answer. At this time pick your pencil up and respond.

11. *Highlight the important words or phrases in each question with your pencil before answering it, or for more emphasis try a highlighter or a pen with a different color of ink.* Underline, circle, or highlight the key or operational words or phrases in each question before answering it.

12. *Understand the difference between a correct answer and the best answer.* This is especially relevant for multiple-choice questions, where there may be more than one correct answer but only one (it is hoped) best answer. Again, understanding the instructor's perceptions and testing style will help.

13. *Budget your time effectively. Always take a watch with you to the exam.* Pace yourself and try to save a few minutes at the end for review. It is important to know where you are in a time sense during an exam to avoid last-minute panic feelings that sweep over you when you realize that you have just ten minutes remaining in which to complete the second half of the exam.

14. *Answer the easy questions first.* This will build up your confidence, allow for better use of your time, and may jog your memory or provide help in answering the hard questions.

15. *Trust your first response.* Don't change your answer unless you have a very good reason to do so. First impressions and answers are not always right, but it is unwise to change your initial answer unless you are certain of the "correctness" of the alternative choice.

16. *Review.* Take a few minutes, or as much time as you have available after finishing your exam, to review your answers. Review first to ensure that you have answered all the necessary questions, to see if anything has been left out or unanswered; then go back to check for the correctness of your responses. Review your problem solutions, if appropriate, to make sure that your numbers are legible and understandable. Put your pencil down when reviewing. Don't change answers unless you are very certain of the alternate responses. (See #15.)

Strategies For Different Types of Exams

There are basically two different types of examinations: "objective" and "subjective." Objective tests come in various forms; e.g., true-false, multiple choice, fill-in-the-blank, matching, and problem solving. These tests are designed to measure your knowledge of facts, formulas, and details. Subjective exams go beyond objective tests and require that you recall facts and ideas and organize them into meaningful sentences and paragraphs. Essay exams are most representative of this form of test. The following suggestions may be helpful when taking different types of exams. *These strategies should accompany, not replace, concerted studying and adequate test preparation.*

True-False Tests

1. Don't assume that the answers follow a certain order or pattern, such as T F T F or T T F F.

2. Attend to every word in the question/statement. Be cautious of words such as "all," "never," "always," "everyone"—they *usually* indicate a false answer. Words such as "frequently," "often," "probably," and "generally" *often* indicate a true answer.

Multiple-Choice Tests

1. Read questions twice before you attempt to answer. Put your pencil down the first time as a safeguard against premature answering. After you have read the complete question and all answer choices, you can pick up your pencil and reread them, ready to make a choice.

2. Read all the answers; even if the first one seems right, another choice may be better, or "all of the above" might be correct.

3. Make sure that the grammatical structure (e.g., subject-verb agreement) of the question and the answer you choose is correct. If it is not, your answer is probably wrong (or the teacher needs help with English grammar). For example:

   College *freshmen* typically

   a. *are* more concerned with academic achievement than with social life. (correct—according to this professor)

   b. *gives* social life higher priority than academic achievement. (incorrect— subject is plural; verb, singular)

4. When in doubt between answers, go with your first impression.

5. Put a check mark or draw a line through each answer you eliminate. Unless instructed or told otherwise, don't be afraid to write on the test. Sometimes writing out answers or completing a chart, diagram, or outline will jog your memory or help to integrate facts, thereby providing the necessary clues to choosing the best answer.

6. The answer to one question is often given in another question. If one question sounds familiar, go back to see if you can find the answer within the test itself. (Be careful that you don't spend too much time going back and forth.)

7. If you are at a complete loss and there is no stated penalty for guessing, choose the longest answer (especially if the teacher has made up the test himself).

8. The more specific the answer is, the more likely it is to be correct.

9. When opposite choices are listed in the group of answers, one of them often is correct.

10. When two choices begin with the same prefix or syllable, or two choices are very similar in meaning, one of them is usually correct. Following are examples:

   A. The primary cause of academic failure by college students is their

      1. overemphasisis of social life

      2. *in*adequate planning of time

      3. *in*sufficient academic background for college work

      4. laziness

   According to this professor, choice 2, which has the same prefix as choice 3, is correct.

   B. Adjustment to college can be difficult for students primarily because:

      1. they tend to have unrealistic expectations about college life

      2. they have not been independent of their parents for extended periods of time

3. they have not yet assumed this much responsibility for their own lives

4. they lack the emotional preparedness necessary for adjustment to college

According to this professor, choice 3, which is similar in meaning to choice 2, is correct.

Fill-in-the-Blank Tests

These tests require that you provide the word or phrase that best completes the statement. One way to study for this type of exam is to organize the information studied into statements as you go along. In other words, think in complete sentences instead of memorizing separate facts. The summary part of the Key and Summary method of lecture note-taking described in Part Two, Chapter 4 may be especially helpful when studying for fill-in-the-blank tests.

Matching Tests

Your task on this type of test is to match one item on a list with another item on a different list; for instance, matching names of famous scientists from one list with their "discoveries" on another list.

Use a basic process-of-elimination approach here—matching the items you are sure of first, then going to the harder ones. Caution: Read the directions carefully to determine if there is a penalty for guessing or to see if any answers can be used more than once.

Problem-Solving Tests

This type of test is very common in mathematics and technology-oriented courses. The best way to study for these tests is to work practice problems until you are confident that you understand how the formula or principle works in all possible cases.

When preparing for tests such as these, spend time connecting concepts with pictures, symbols, formulas, diagrams, etc. Try to link general concepts with the specific examples given in class or in your text. Attempt to connect new knowledge with that which was previously learned. Think of real-world examples and words to describe mathematical or scientific words, concepts, or symbols.

Learn to use many different modes—visual, imaginal, experiential—to flesh out and connect new principles and knowledge. Meaningfulness (and your subsequent ability to encode and retrieve this information) is increased when information is interconnected. Retrieval is increased as these interconnections are strengthened through practice and repeated use. Review the learning strategies presented in Part Two, Chapter 7 on memory if you need help with study techniques for this type of test.

Solve sample problems in your texts and/or problem sets given on homework assignments; then attempt to create your own questions connecting the concepts to be learned. You may find forming study groups and dividing the number of questions among group members a practical and time-saving approach. Be careful, however, to make sure that each group member takes the time to explain the solution in a way you will understand. Don't rush through this part of the study process—and *remember, the responsibility for what you learn is on you, not the other group members.* So ask questions and demand clear answers.

Demonstration Tests

In lab courses you may be asked to show the lab instructor what you know, such as preparing a slide or assembling a circuit. The best way to study for this type of test is to practice in a real, "hands-on" way. Schedule extra lab time and practice doing the things that you will be expected to know (perform) in a demonstration exam.

Identification Tests

Another type of exam frequently used in science lab courses is the test in which you are shown a number of specimens and are asked to identify and/or provide information about them. The best way to prepare is to memorize the most important distinguishing characteristics of each item.

Open-Book Tests

Your professor may give you this type of exam because she wants you to prepare well-crafted answers that, because of in-class time limits, might not be possible under normal testing situations. Organization, style, grammar, and punctuation are very important, so take extra care not only in what you say but in how you say it. Students who do well with take-home exams usually spend considerably more time with them than the professor suggests.

A variation of this type of exam is the take-home type containing a number of questions from which the professor will select one or two for you to answer in class (without notes). In this case it may be sufficient for you simply to outline your answers to every question, or you may find it necessary to write them out completely. *I cannot overstress the fact that a response should be prepared for every question— don't risk trying to outguess the professor and attempt to figure out which of the questions will be on the test.* If there are too many questions for you to answer for the given time constraints, form a study group and divide up the questions. Make sure you have, and spend, sufficient time going over the other group members' answers—and get copies of them. Add facts or information of your own to these answers so the professor knows that it is your answer and is not copied from someone else's work.

Essay Tests

A good general suggestion for preparing for essay tests is to take time before the exam to anticipate the questions that might appear on it. *Develop your own practice essay questions by looking over your lecture notes and text and trying to identify the key points and main ideas of each.* Then consider what questions your professor may select and write out a variety of responses, in outline form, for each. Study these outlined responses before the real test. It also may be helpful to answer any discussion questions or sample essay questions provided by your instructor or by the text.

Here are some specific strategies for succeeding at essay tests:

1. Read the directions carefully and *underline the "action" words*; e.g., compare, discuss, define, contrast, etc. These key words tell you what to do, and each requires a different type of response. "Compare" means to show the similarities and differences between things; "contrast" means to indicate the differences. "Describe" means to give details or descriptions. "Justify" asks you to give supporting arguments, while "enumerate" simply means to list the main reasons, events, or facts. "Evaluate" requires that you give the pros and cons of something and your own opinions on the issue in question.

    Also note if the directions ask for specific numbers of responses; e.g., three reasons, four causes or sentences, words or paragraphs. Determine whose point of view (yours, the teacher's, the text's) is wanted. Do the directions indicate an order or sequence in which the facts should be written? Underline all the key words that let you know exactly the form, content, and intent of your response.

2. Before writing your response, analyze the time allotment and budget your time accordingly. Two well-thought-out, although incomplete, responses may be better than one complete essay and one left untried (or vice versa). Talk with your professor beforehand and discuss this issue; his response will be helpful in budgeting your time.

3. Briefly outline your answer before writing it. Keep your outline to the point and simple; fill in details as you write the essay. Number your major ideas in the order in which you will write them in your answer. Circle any idea for which you plan to give an example or detailed illustration. (If you find you did not have enough time to develop each answer as fully as possible, you might consider handing in your outline as well as your written essay. You might be able to use this as evidence proving how much you really know.)

4. Write a well-structured, organized essay that focuses on the question. Typically, students' responses are too general and include too much "padding." Don't add extraneous words or ideas just to fill out the essay so it looks as though you have something to say. Quantity is not necessarily quality, and a careful reader will soon discover this.

   Another common weakness of essays is the "choppiness" in which ideas are presented. Sentences should flow together into a coherent whole. You need to *focus on and use transition words* that enable the relationship between sentences, paragraphs, and thoughts to be demonstrated. Practice using the following transition words in your essays:

Therefore	Consequently	In addition
First	Of course	However
Second	Finally	As a result
Also	Next	Nevertheless
Moreover	Thus	In summary

5. Organize your response in a hierarchical way following a 1-3-1 or keyhole pattern. (See Chapter 10 for a more complete description of this.) In your first paragraph the question should be restated in your own words as an introduction to the task at hand. Follow this by your general answer, thesis, or main point. This section should contain at least three key ideas that need further clarification. Develop and support each of these ideas fully in three separate paragraphs. These

paragraphs should include the facts and supporting documentation that will reinforce the main point made in the introductory paragraph. Finally, a conclusion paragraph should be written restating the question and your answer.

Chapter 10 includes detailed suggestions for improving your writing skills, and you might consider jumping ahead to this section at this time.

6. Check your paper before you hand it in. Depending upon the time remaining, make sure you:

    a. answered all parts of the question as indicated by the directions

    b. did what each question asked you to do

    c. answered the correct number of questions

    d. checked for spelling, punctuation, grammar, factual mistakes and omitted words and phrases. (Sometimes your mind moves faster than your pencil and you leave some words out.)

Chapter 9

MANAGE TEST ANXIETY

Notes

Your performance on a test may not always be an accurate reflection of your intelligence, effort or study behaviors. Ineffective handling of the pressures of testing situations can disrupt your performance on tests and lead to lower scores. Test anxiety is common and can have a negative influence on grades.

Test anxiety adversely affects your feelings about yourself and about the testing situation and can lead you to engage in negative thinking. These negative thoughts, in turn, can lead you to expect lower grades and to believe that you are less prepared than you really are. Negative thoughts result in test-anxious students getting grades lower than those of nontest-anxious students.

Anxiety is a negative factor in that it interferes with normal mental functioning and has an adverse influence on almost every aspect of school achievement. Specific anxiety reactions to test situations differ, but most students can be helped to overcome negative anxiety effects.

Time for a little self-assessment now. Take a few minutes to read and think about each of the following statements. Do any of the following descriptions fit the way you feel or behave before a test? Rank them in order: 1—most like me, to 3—you must be kidding, not like me at all.

- Cramming the night before the test, feeling panicky. A night of restless sleep resulting in a feeling of exhaustion the morning of the exam. Tension as you walk into the classroom worrying about whether a section of material you didn't study will be covered on the test. A confused, "tight" feeling in your brain as the answers to the questions become harder and harder to select. Rank _____

- A slight bit of "helpful anxiety" as you review previously studied material the night before the exam. No cramming—just refreshing yourself on the material to be tested. Anxiety slightly higher than usual, but not enough to interfere with your performance on the test.

Rank _____

- Little motivation to study. Although you know that the exam is important, you just can't seem to get yourself to sit down and study. You feel disturbingly calm, considering the fact that you have studied very little for this exam. You clean your room, do laundry, or anything instead of studying.

    Rank _____

None of the previous descriptions may completely capture the way *you* manage your test anxiety, but they are examples of the many styles people exhibit in coping with test anxiety. Obviously, some coping styles are more effective than others, and I would guess that the second scenario described would result in the best test performance of the three.

Take a moment to consider your typical coping style. How do you show your tension? _____

_____

What triggers this response? _____

_____

What do you do with this stress? _____

_____

Do you suffer from any stress-related problems, such as headaches, nervous stomach, or muscle tightness? _____

_____

This *first step to effective management of test anxiety—understanding your own personal signs and symptoms of anxiety*—may be the most difficult for some. Awareness of negative stress responses may not be very high because of the learned expectation that tests "should" make us feel "crazy," anxious, and "stressed out." We may have learned to think that test anxiety is in fact a normal response to an abnormal situation, not the other way around!

You can learn to identify your own stress symptoms and to reduce the negative stress reactions in ways that can lead to better studying and better test performance. *Effective management of test anxiety involves modification of attitudes and behaviors during the pretest situations and during the actual, live, "for real" test-taking experience.*

Managing Pretest Anxiety

Often, as an exam nears, you may feel overwhelmed by the work yet to be done and may tend to avoid studying, study quickly without really learning anything, or feel so panicked that you can't concentrate. Some of the following tips may help you avoid or reduce these negative feelings and actions:

1. *Break overwhelming tasks down into smaller, more manageable tasks.* Just as a marathon runner may find it easier to think of running 12 two-mile runs than one 26-mile ordeal, you may find it less difficult to read three 20-page sections than one 60-page assignment.

   Make a list of "Tasks to be Done" and try to build a sense of accomplishment by successfully completing a number of small steps that lead to the larger goal. This may include chapters to be read, chapters to be reviewed, a talk with your T.A., practice on an old exam, and material to be reviewed only if time allows. Spread your studying out over several days. In this way you can learn smaller amounts of information in each study session. The quantity of material will be more manageable and easier to encode into your memory banks. The result will be a decrease in anxiety as your goal for each study session is achieved. You are in this way reducing mountains to molehills!

2. *Play being teacher and student.* Construct and answer questions that might be asked on the exam. This helps you focus on what you do know. It also might be helpful to review guidelines on how to take specific tests. (See Part 2, Chapter 8, Play [and Win] the Test "Game.")

3. *Monitor your worrying.* If you begin to worry excessively, use this as a cue to stop worrying. Worrying is understandable, but it is not helpful. It keeps you from focusing on the material to be studied. When you find that worrying is not constructive, take a deep breath and let the air out slowly in order to relax. Do this a few times, and then focus your attention on the task at hand. Practicing this periodically will help you control your anxiety and enable you to work more effectively.

Worry can also be reduced by developing a mental attitude that seeks out and destroys the irrational roots of the worrying thoughts. You may be able to reduce worry by following some or all of the following suggestions developed by Albert Ellis and Robert Harper (1976).

a. Convince yourself that worrying about the outcome of your test will aggravate the situation, not improve it.

b. Try not to exaggerate the importance or significance of the test. Identify the short- and long-term consequences of the test accurately. Ask your professor what the test "really" means in grading and in the "grand scheme of things."

c. Accept the fact that a negative test score may prove inconvenient, annoying, disappointing and unfortunate, but rarely is it ever as terrible or awful as it first seems.

d. Examine and challenge your internal thoughts and beliefs; ask where these come from. Question yourself: "Why would it be so awful if I do badly on this test?"; "Would it really be so terrible if. . ."

e. Realize that many fears are a disguised form of the "fear of disapproval." Learn to challenge this fear. Identify whose disapproval you fear. Ask yourself what this disapproval really means. Is disapproval the same as rejection? Can you realistically expect the approval of all people all the time?

4. *Think about your own standards of success and failure.* Quite often the problem of pretest anxiety is connected to the attitudes and feelings that students bring with them to the testing situation. Many students develop a "specter of failure" and bring this with them to the test. The feeling is that despite one's intelligence and hard work one is bound to do poorly. This *anticipation of failure often develops into a fear of failure, which in turn creates anxiety and can lead to poor performance—the very outcome feared.*

Failure itself is a subjective outcome meaning different things to different people. For high-achieving students failure does not necessarily mean getting an F on an exam or in a course. Standards may be set so high that only As and Bs are acceptable and even a C is viewed as a failure. If you need to be the best in the class, then getting an A can still be experienced as a failure if other students get higher grades.

Are your own standards of success and failure reasonable? Are you asking of yourself something that you really want, or have these needs been externally imposed upon you by others (parents, friends, teachers, etc.) and internalized over time? Are you pushing yourself for grades that you are honestly, realistically capable of attaining; are your goals reasonable and rational? Are you really being fair to yourself?

5. *Analyze the consequences of failure.* Look at failure head-on in realistic terms—what are the real consequences of failing a test, a course, or college in general? Probably for many of you failure at any of these would be perceived as dreadful—your life would feel less worth living and your future tainted if you failed. But is this really so?

People do not think in reasonable terms when considering failure. We tend to blow the importance of failure out of proportion, become unduly pessimistic and self-defeating when faced with the prospect of failure. I suggest that you analyze your feelings about failure and attempt to determine if you are excessive with the importance you attach to avoiding it. What would really happen if you failed calculus, or psychology, or flunked out of college altogether? Would all your chances for future happiness cease? Or would it simply be a battle lost with the war ahead still winnable?

One way to combat this fear of failure is to give yourself permission to fail (sounds weird but is often true). Give yourself the freedom *not* to live up to some arbitrary standard of success. Look at failure for what it is, not what you emotionally (and irrationally) expect it to be. Learn to disassociate your *self* from your *performance.* You are a "person" and ultimately more than success vs. failure. Your self-worth and dignity go beyond how well you do on a test or in school. Giving yourself freedom to fail is a sign of respect for and acceptance of yourself. It illustates that you think well of yourself no matter what you do on a test or in a course.

Giving yourself freedom to fail often results in success. It frees you from the burden and pressure to perform and the anxiety that this pressure produces.

6. *Accept that striving to be your best may not yield perfection, and that's O.K.* Remember, you have limitations, natural and learned. You can't be perfect at all things at all times. The need to be perfect is unrealistic and represents an unsatisfiable goal that is sure to produce anxiety. Keep telling yourself that *wanting* to be the best is good;

needing to be the best will frequently lead to undue stress. Now repeat after me: *"I want to strive to be my best; I don't need to be the best!"*

7. *Keep attacking in a rational way previously conquered worries and fears that temporarily return,* looking for—and casting out— negative, irrational, self-defeating thoughts and anxieties.

Managing Anxiety During the Exam

Your ability to manage anxiety during an exam is of critical importance for success. Note that I use the word "manage." Some anxiety during an exam, often referred to as "functional" anxiety, can actually help you to perform well. It serves as an energizer and motivator, which can help in focusing your attention. *Your goal is not to eliminate anxiety but to control it, to learn to harness its energy and make it work for, not against you,* so that it does not interfere with your performance on the exam.

If you begin to tense up during an exam, try some of the following suggestions:

1. Try to *be aware of the negative thoughts* and things that you might be saying to yourself. These internal self-statements often increase anxiety. Examples include "Everybody else seems to be writing faster than I am," or "I must be stupid if I can't figure out this problem," or "I don't want to be the last one done." These kinds of thoughts keep you focused on areas irrelevant to the test itself, are distractions, and serve only to increase your anxiety.

2. Once you've identified the negative statements you have been thinking, refocus your attention on the question or problem you are trying to answer.

3. *Take time out!* Most students can spare 30-60 seconds during a test to sit back, take a breath, and relax. This break can help to control anxiety, freshen the mind, and improve performance for the remainder of the test.

4. *Practice Relaxation Techniques.* Quite often when you are tense, you not only feel that tension emotionally but also tend to tense your muscles without being aware of it. People tend to tense different muscle groups. Some feel the tension at the backs of their necks, others in their stomachs, and still others along their jaws. If they can relax physically, people are often also able to relax emotionally. How do you experience tension and stress? Take a few moments and write

down your physical stress responses.

_____

_____

_____

_____

_____

Sometimes before an exam you may feel so tense that sleeping is impossible—and the harder you try to sleep, the more frustrating it becomes. One way to relieve tension is by tightening and then relaxing the specific muscle groups that feel tense. This has the double benefit of relaxing you physically and taking your mind off the stress-producing thoughts, focusing on relaxing the muscles.

Try this, for example: Tense your right hand, forearm, and bicep by making a fist. Tense it very hard. Feel the tightness and the pulling. Tense for a few seconds until it feels quite uncomfortable. Now relax your fist, your fingers, and your forearm. Notice the relief and calm in that part of your body. Feel the warmth or tingling feeling in your arm. Notice the difference between tension and relaxation.

You may try this with any muscle group (or combination of muscle groups). Tense—and then relax. Focus on the muscles.

Sometimes, especially when you don't have time to do muscle relaxation (such as when you are actually sitting taking your test), the following simple breathing exercise may help you relax.

Deep Breathing Exercise

Close your eyes and take a slow, deep breath; then slowly exhale. Continue doing this slowly, paying attention to your lungs slowly filling with air and then slowly emptying as you relax. Each time you exhale, repeat the word "one" silently (or repeat another word that may have some relaxation value for you, such as "warm" or "calm"). Each time you exhale, allow yourself to relax further. When you feel calm again, and you should be able to achieve this after 30-60 seconds with practice, open your eyes and resume work.

Test anxiety can be controlled and its negative impact upon your test performance minimized. Anxiety management skills must be learned; they do not come naturally for most people. Thankfully, they are not difficult to learn, and you can improve your ability to reduce pretest anxiety as well as the nervousness that occurs during the testing situation. Changing mental attitudes in combination with learning to control body stress reactions will increase your likelihood of academic success.

Chapter 10

IMPROVE YOUR WRITING SKILLS

Writing is a tool for thinking and learning. In addition to enabling you to uncover and understand new ideas, writing allows you to communicate with and extend your knowledge to others. You write to comprehend, question, interpret, summarize, criticize, support, analyze, synthesize, as well as to create. Writing assignments will vary during your course of studies, but you certainly will be asked to perform some, if not all, of these writing functions.

Writing is a fact of life for college students. A term paper, essay, lab report, or some other form of written expression will be required at various points along the way. This is true no matter what your major. Academic success is dependent upon your ability to locate, collect, organize, and communicate ideas and facts in written as well as spoken forms.

All students, those in engineering and technological majors as well as those in liberal arts, need to attend to and improve their writing. It has been estimated, for example, that 80 percent of a beginning engineer's job time will be spent communicating with colleagues and only 20 percent doing technological work that directly utilizes engineering skills. Much of this communication involves writing reports, memos, and professional correspondence. Good writing is essential even for those students who live in the world of numbers and scientific formulas!

The ability to write effectively not only relates to academic success while in college but transfers to job success later on in the real world. Just ask any corporate recruiter about the importance of writing. I will guarantee that the response given will emphasize the necessity of having effective writing ability at the time of hiring and for advancement up the corporate ladder.

The Research Paper

Writing research papers is at the very heart of academic life. The intellectual activity that is part and parcel of college learning is built upon the scholarly investigation and sharing of ideas and information. The research paper represents the method and medium for this activity, and it is difficult to imagine not writing at least one during your college career.

There are five commonly assigned types of research papers. Each requires a different style of writing. These varieties can be classified by the amount of creative effort required of the author. The five types of papers are listed in order of complexity and need for author creativity and involvement; 1 is the simplest and 5, the most complex.

1. *The Report*—involves a summary or synopsis of someone else's work, can occasionally require some synthesis and evaluation.

2. *The Review of Research*—requires paraphrasing, abstraction, and summarizing.

3. *The Directive Essay*—involves specifying technical order and/or directions, process analysis, or division/classification.

4. *The Problem/Solution Essay*—combines synthesis, directive, and process analysis. The writer is usually required to provide probable and possible solution or resolution to a stated problem.

5. *The Argument*—requires the most creative effort. The writer must provide support and evidence to augment a certain thesis or hypothesis.

The first step in writing a good paper is to clarify the nature of the task. It is vital that you understand the professor's instructions and be clear as to the type of paper required. If you are uncertain about what type of paper you are to write, or about specific requirements such as length, punctuation, and style format, ask the professor for clarification before you begin. Let me repeat—before you begin!

The paper-writing process can be divided into three phases: Prewriting; Research; and Writing.

Prewriting

The *Prewriting* phase represents the foundation upon which your paper is built. As in any construction project, a hastily built and poorly anchored structure will not pass inspection by the building inspector or support the weight and ravages of time. It is important to establish the parameters of your project, to identify the sources of your building materials before you grab the shovel and begin digging.

This phase includes the following activities:

A. Choosing a topic

B. Identifying resources: discovering where to go

C. Understanding how to use resources

In *choosing a topic* it is important that you select a subject that will interest you and, it is hoped, the professor. It is wise to avoid new or state-of-the-art topic areas unless you are sure that there are sufficient references available or unless you are specifically instructed to do so.

When choosing a topic, it may be helpful for you to consider and answer the following questions:

1. What type of paper should I, must I, write?

2. What is the specific topic?

3. Is the topic of sufficient/necessary depth, breadth, or focus? (In writing a paper, it is my opinion that a well-developed, well-written paper on a clearly, yet narrowly, defined topic is superior to a paper that is too broad and overly ambitious.) In other words, unless your professor specifically requests otherwise, attempt to define a narrow question/topic and develop it fully.

4. How is the topic different, unique, or special compared to those chosen by others in the class?

5. What are the component parts, the subtopics?

6. Does your topic focus on a particular stage in its development? What is happening in the area now; how has it changed; where is it going?

7. Who/what does it affect? What are its outcomes?

8. What good is it? How can topic be evaluated?

9. Are there ethical, legal, economic, political, social, psychological, technological issues involved?

As an alternative, try this: Audio tape yourself saying whatever you can think of about the subjects you choose to write about. Follow the question format just described and tape-record your responses. After verbally brainstorming in this way, replay the tape a few times to pick out the key ideas. Hearing, coupled with writing and thinking, helps you to develop and clarify your topics and provides better structure for the research and writing stages that follow. Why not give this approach a try?

After asking yourself these questions, it is important to attempt to *identify and investigate the resources* available to you for use in researching your topic.

It is critical for you to *become familiar with your campus or community library or libraries.* Many libraries have guided tours to familiarize users with available services; swallow your pride and take advantage of one. Speak to the reference librarian and/or read any printed pamphlets describing reference resources before committing yourself to a topic.

Inquire about how to *do a computerized literature search* if such a service is available. This "high tech" aid can be an invaluable timesaving device. Most college libraries now are equipped with a computerized on-line search service that can be used to obtain references from journal articles and other needed sources of information. The library's designated on-line searcher will work with you to identify search topics and to formulate a plan to extract information from one or more computerized data bases. Then, utilizing a microcomputer, the searcher can "talk" to the data bases through the telephone network. There are over 200 data bases available in nearly every subject area. *The bibliography at the end of this book contains a partial list of frequently accessed data bases in various disciplines.* Obviously, it is essential to focus on and define your search topic as quickly and clearly as possible, making your library on-line consultant an especially important resource. You don't have to be intimidated by computer technology either, as on-line search procedures are simple and, for most students today, easy to follow.

It may also be helpful during the prewriting stage to learn about interlibrary loan procedures. This program connects your library with many others, expanding its holdings greatly, thereby increasing your potential list of resources.

Many, if not most, college libraries today have learning resource, study skills, or writing skills centers available to students. These can be valuable resources. Such centers provide professional staff members who can help with the prewriting as well as with the research and writing stages. In fact, these staff members may have more time available to help you than does the librarian, and they have appropriate resources at their disposal.

You may find it helpful to discuss your topic with your professor and seek his assistance in locating possible information sources. In this regard, a professor's bookshelf is often useful for more than collecting dust! On it there just might be a key reference to get you focused and started on your way.

As you are getting started, it may also be helpful to check the bibliography or reference section of a few key books, periodicals, or journal articles for listings of other possible sources.

One last point—check the credentials of the author(s) of your sources as well as you can. It could be very helpful to know the level of expertise or qualifications of your references before you assign authority status to them. It may be inappropriate, for example, to use a convicted embezzler as an expert on finance ethics.

Research

After identifying a topic, your *next step is to collect the material* with which to construct the framework and support the actual building (writing) process.

When considering sources for a paper, expand your view to include a wide range of reference material. Don't focus on just one or two information formats such as books and journals. Consider additional sources such as: encyclopedia, television programs, radio and film productions, computer software, illustrations, and political cartoons.

Books can be located by using the card catalog in your library. To efficiently use the subject entries in the card catalog, it might be helpful for you first to consult the *Library of Congress Subject Headings,* which usually is found near the catalog. In this endeavor, as in all aspects of library use, the librarian stands ready to help. It probably would be a good first step to read any material that your library has prepared (and almost all have something) to orient users to library services and location of resources. If some of the information you seek is unavailable in your campus libraries, ask the librarian about intercampus loans or interuniversity walk-in borrowing privileges.

The on-line search service previously mentioned can be an invaluable resource during the initial research stage. Review the prewriting section in this chapter and the bibliography at this time for additional information.

You may prefer not to use this on-line search service but, instead, to review printed index sources. Printed indexes abound, covering almost all subject areas. They are stored in the reference section in your library, and this area should become well-known to you before your academic career is finished (or, should I say, completed!) The bibliography at the end of this book also contains a selected listing of indexes and reference guides in various subject areas. Consulting this listing may be helpful in conducting your initial research.

Writing

After choosing and researching your topic, the next stage is putting your thoughts and facts on paper. Writing, for most college students, is still the most basic way of illustrating what you know.

The newest movement in the teaching of writing in the United States today emphasizes the writing *process*, not the *product*. Following this trend, I encourage you to write your thoughts and ideas without worrying about making technical mistakes (at least during the initial stages of writing). Grammar, spelling, and structure are dealt with *after* you have had the opportunity to expose your inner self. The fine details are put on *after* the essential ideas are presented. This approach attempts to reduce the fear of making mistakes by focusing on the free flow of ideas.

I believe that this approach can be helpful for most students, and I would like to suggest *four specific steps to improve your writing*. In addition to stimulating writing creativity, I believe that these suggestions will also refocus attention and responsibility from teacher to student. As I have stated many times, you can maximize your chances for academic success by accepting personal responsibility for the learning process and learning outcomes.

1. *The first step in this writing process, immediately following the prewriting and research phases, is called DRAFTING.* Write a first draft of your paper without worrying about structure, spelling, or grammar. The goal is to produce a "hard copy" of your thoughts and ideas in a form that can be similar to brainstorming. (Of course, the "hard copy" can also be on the hard drive or floppy diskette of your word processor).

2. *After this has been accomplished, the feedback process can be begun by SHARING what you have written with others.* Whom you share with depends upon many variables: type of assignment availability of classmates roommate cooperation, and so forth. What's important at this stage is for you to share your written work so that your peers and/ or teachers can question you and comment on what you have written. A powerful way to share your writing is to read it out loud. It may

take some courage for you to do this, but I believe your writing will improve greatly as a result. It is often easier for others to respond verbally than it is for them to write out their responses. In this way feedback will be immediate and will not delay your writing efforts.

It is important for you not to react defensively to the feedback offered. *Remember, this is only your first draft, not your finished product.* Record these responses and be prepared to incorporate them into the next draft.

3. *The third step in the writing process involves REVISING your first draft based partly on the shared feedback.* Expand ideas, clarify confusion, fill in incomplete sections, and reorganize information as necessary. Include whatever feedback you think helps make your paper better.

4. *FINAL EDITING does not take place until after step three is completed.* Now you focus on eliminating mechanical and grammatical errors. I encourage you to do as much of your own proofreading and editing as possible. As a practical matter, the choice of correct spelling and word usage may be facilitated with a word processor. Efficient editing will be stimulated because you can focus your attention on this mechanical task and not be sidetracked into formulating new ideas or creating new phrases or text.

Revision is the key element in this writing process. I encourage you to write, get something down on paper, and worry about it making sense later on. *First, DO IT; then later, FIX IT!* If you know that your first draft will be revised later on, the pressure of writing is lifted. Revision is not punishment but a necessary and logical part of good writing.

The structure of the essay or paper is the base upon which your writing is built. Structure is refined during the revision part of the writing process. *Structure* represents *a logical sequence of ideas* presented to support your position or to state your case. Writing your paper in a structured, ordered way is essential to good writing. It is not, however, a skill that seems to come easily for most college students.

It is easier to write good sentences than to construct cohesive, flowing paragraphs. College students seem to be more successful in writing sentences that present ideas in a limited, "stand-alone" fashion. Writing to present details and stringing them along in poorly connected sentence after sentence is characteristic of many college students.

You can learn to develop the ability to write well-constructed sentences that flow together to produce strong paragraphs by following a structured writing formula or format.

The need for order, for a structured pattern in which to organize your written words, is true for students in all majors. Engineering students, as well as those in liberal arts, require clear paths along which their written ideas can travel. Such a path has an identifiable beginning, middle, and end.

Sheridan Baker in *The Practical Stylist with Readings* (1982) illustrates clearly this need for structure.

> You need a clear beginning to give your essay character and direction so the reader can tell where he is going and can look forward with expectation. Your beginning, of course, will set forth your thesis. You need a middle to amplify and fulfill. This will be the body of your argument, the bulk of your essay. You need an end to let readers know that they have arrived and where . . .
>
> Give your essay the three-part feel of beginning, middle, and end—the mind likes this triple order. Many a freshman's essay has no structure and leaves no impression. It is all chaotic middle. It has no beginning, it just starts; it has no end, it just stops, fagged out at two in the morning. (p. 31)

This same beginning, middle, end structure can be followed when writing a term paper as well as a shorter essay. Instead of the beginning and end being limited to one paragraph each in an essay, you can take more space and use more thoughts in building and closing a multipage research report or term paper.

The Keyhole Format

You can learn a useful and simple format that, if followed, will enable you to write clear, well-organized compositions. The format gets its name from its keyhole shape and can help you unlock the secrets to successful essay and paper writing. The Keyhole Format is presented in Figure 20.

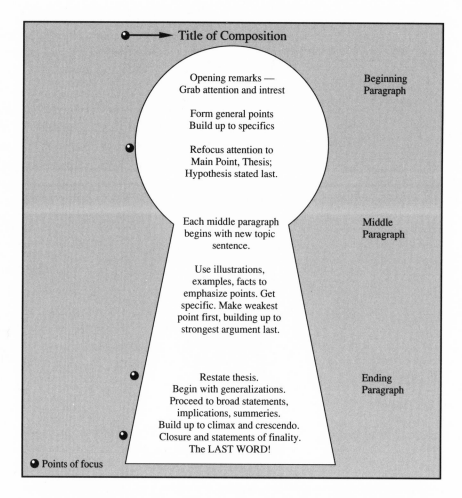

Figure 20. The Keyhole Format: A Suggested Structure for Written Compositions. Adapted from *The Practical Stylist with Readings* (5th ed.) by S. Baker, 1982, New York: Harper & Row.

The shape of this diagram illustrates the structural framework proposed: an identifiable beginning, middle, and end. In addition, the building up, rounding out, and generalizing function of each part is also easily seen. The beginning includes the opening statements and presentation of the main thesis of your paper. Arrange your main points in increasing order of interest and importance. In other words, end the beginning part of your paper with the most critical point. The reader's attention and interest should build up, ascending to the key sentence.

You may find it difficult to do this. Students often present their best points first, those that they are most sure of, and then let their statements fizzle out, using "filler" to take up space. The reader's interest is thereby left to decline instead of build up, and the writing lacks punch and effect.

This same crescendo effect—building up to a dynamic climax—is recommended when writing the middle part of your paper. The weaker arguments are presented first, leading up to the strongest.

Use a similar format for each paragraph, whereby each presents an equal image to the reader. Attempt to use a similar number of sentences per paragraph, say four or five, so that each feels like an orderly building block, structurally sound and solid. Doing this may encourage a "structural rhythm" and sense of balance that is helpful in both writing and reading the text. Once accustomed to this structure you can vary the rhythm and length of your paragraphs as a means of emphasis, calling attention to key points when desired.

Attention needs to be given while writing this middle part to the construction and use of transitions between paragraphs. Transitions are links, connections between thoughts or ideas presented in subsequent passages. There are many ways to do this: repeat a word or phrase from the preceding paragraph; complete an unfinished idea or statement left dangling; or use common transitional words such as but, however, therefore, nonetheless, of course, instead, etc.

The ending part of your essay or paper is, in a way, an upside-down funnel in which ideas presented in the beginning are reintroduced and elaborated upon. The end starts small and finishes big. The narrow thesis is presented first, and it is reinforced with increasingly impressive statements and stronger generalizations. Implications are broadened, coming from the middle part, building toward closure and a sense of finality and completeness. Your final sentence is your clincher, the summary statement that puts it all to rest. The longer the paper, the more specific the summary of points you have made must be. Short essays may require little or no specific summaries—the restated thesis and broadened implications may be enough.

This whole writing process reminds me of baseball. Baseball? Well, yes, specifically the pitching rotation. A successful baseball team (like a successful essay) must have a corps of competent starters, middle relievers, and stoppers. The starter begins the game and tries to establish a forceful rhythm to the game. He tries to set the theme and to control the game's process and final outcome. Middle relievers are the unglorified members of the pitching staff. They toil the middle innings, trying to regain control of the pace of the game by making the outs in support of the starter's statement. Every baseball team these days needs an effective short-relief man to come in at the end of the game to put the finishing touches on, to save the game. He attempts to "sew things up," to "clinch" the game. His are the last words, telling the story of victory or defeat, Hero or Goat, A or C!

Styles for punctuation, footnoting, and bibliography are becoming more standardized in college these days. The trend seems to be toward shorter forms and simpler styles. The bibliography lists some commonly accepted writing style guides and the disciplines in which they are most often used. Kate Turabian's *A Manual for Writers of Term Papers, Theses, and Dissertations* (1973) is one standard general guide used in many American colleges and universities today. *Reporting Technical Information, 6th Edition,* Houp & Pearsall (1987) is acknowledged as the standard guide for use in scientific and technical writing.

The use of word processors has recently revolutionized writing by including computer software packages programmed with correct punctuation and spelling usages. These word processing programs are readily accessible on college campuses, where most will have computer labs. Becoming friendly with your computer is almost an essential fact of life for today's college student!

A Few Words about Plagiarism

The failure to document or to properly give credit for an idea, fact, or phrase borrowed from another author is plagiarism, a form of theft. Many college students are unaware of the proper definition and scope of plagiarism and, because of laziness or ignorance, inadvertently fall into careless borrowing. Acknowledgment of another author's words, ideas, or information is required if they are original or unique to that author.

Material that falls within the common or public domain—well-known facts, proverbs, quotations that are common knowledge—needs no documentation or attribution as to source. The famous quotation, "Don't fire until you see the whites of their eyes," or the term "yuppie" both fall within the bounds of common knowledge and need no reference. However, any original information or phrase requires a mention of source. You must cite the source if you are actually using another author's words and even if you are using only the writer's ideas.

A basic rule of thumb is: *When in doubt, reference*. The basic nature of research papers is such that you will be gathering information from other sources and then summarizing, synthesizing, abstracting, comparing, evaluating, etc. Therefore, it stands to reason that you will need to document and reference often. The more novel or new and the less you know about your topic, the more frequent should be your citation of proper ownership of information.

Caution is my final word. Be aware of what you borrow and what you create. Avoid inadvertent "stealing" of someone else's efforts and learn to document accurately. When you get to the writing stage, you may wish to ask your professor for additional information or references about plagiarism. Ask for a written definition and check into what the experts say about the topic. Books dealing with writing often will contain detailed descriptions and examples of proper and improper referencing. It might be worth the time and effort to be clear about documentation procedures at the beginning rather than to suffer the consequences of plagiarism when it really counts.

CONCLUSION

Studying consists, for the most part, of private, self-directed, self-managed activities intended to enhance learning and academic success (Thomas & Rohwer, 1986). Study effectiveness represents an interaction between course characteristics (e.g., subject matter, test difficulty, tasks required, teacher performance) and individual characteristics; e.g., ability, experience, sense of personal control, motivation levels, diet and health factors, study conditions, reading and notetaking abilities, test-taking skill. The intent of *The College Success Book: A Whole-Student Approach to Academic Excellence* has been to equip you, the student, with information relevant to the aspects of studying that can be directly influenced and controlled. I have attempted to provide tangible strategies to enhance academic success as well as a clear backdrop of information about the multiple facets of human learning.

I have tried to be specific and general, focused and holistic. I have presented information not found in most study skills texts. The material dealing with diet and the effects of light upon performance are examples of this approach.

My objective in doing this has been to illustrate the multifaceted nature of studying and human learning. In this way I also hope to provide many avenues for intervention and opportunities for improvement. The more activities attempted or strategies utilized, the more effective your study improvement process will become.

As a result of your experiences with this book, I hope you are able to accept a greater degree of personal control over the acquisition, maintenance, and generalization of learning strategies. The type of student I hope to produce is one who can accurately understand the demands of each course and who develops a multidimensional repertoire of study methods and uses it skillfully across different types of courses. This ideal student eventually can generalize these skills to lifelong learning situations. This student will desire educational opportunities where learning is challenging and where he or she will be turned on to taking personal responsibility for meeting these challenges.

It is my sincere hope and belief that this ideal student can, in fact, be you!

It may be helpful as a summary activity to retake the *Academic Skills Inventory*, first presented in the Introduction, at this time. Compare your results; I hope you will notice improvement in your study behavior. Remember, this inventory is not a scientific evaluation but a tool for you to focus on the many interrelated components that lead to academic success.

ACADEMIC SKILLS INVENTORY

	Rarely or Never	Some-times	Often or Always

A. GENERAL STUDY HABITS & ATTITUDES

1. I approach each course with the attitude that my grade is primarily the result of my effort and ability, not luck or what the professor does _____ _____ _____

2. I begin each course with the expectation that I will do well _____ _____ _____

3. I set reachable, realistic goals for each course _____ _____ _____

4. When determining what to work on first, I write down a list of priorities and start with the most important task _____ _____ _____

5. I make time for exercise even during the busiest times of the school year _____ _____ _____

6. I am aware of my eating habits and maintain a balanced diet _____ _____ _____

7. I have a hard time controlling stress and nervousness _____ _____ _____

8. I do most of my studying at night and find myself tired in the morning _____ _____ _____

9. I have a clear sense of what my career is going to be after I finish college _____ _____ _____

10. I approach each course as unique and develop study plans tailored just for it _____ _____ _____

11. Before each class meets I spend a few minutes thinking about what will be discussed _____ _____ _____

12. My study approach emphasizes active involvement— doing as much as I can to learn _____ _____ _____

	Rarely or Never	Some-times	Often or Always

B. *READING EFFECTIVENESS*

13. I preview the material before reading

14. I read the material to get it finished as quickly as possible

15. I underline, highlight, or take notes as I read

16. Immediately after reading, I review and recheck to make sure I understand

C. *NOTE-TAKING*

17. I have trouble anticipating what the lecture will cover

18. I sit in the back half of the classroom

19. I miss important points in the lecture because I'm too busy taking notes

20. I spend a few minutes immediately after class reviewing my notes

D. *TIME MANAGEMENT*

21. My study periods are often too long and I find myself getting bored or easily distracted

22. I write out a study schedule for the entire term so I can see the "big picture"

23. I find it difficult to do work in advance and get caught up in cram sessions to beat the deadline

24. I set up a study schedule that allows me to study every course every day

	Rarely or Never	Some-times	Often or Always

E. STUDY ENVIRONMENT

25. I eat when I study

26. Near my desk I have photographs of loved ones

27. I study with a radio or stereo on

28. I study at a place that I reserve for studying only

F. CONCENTRATION

29. I find it difficult to block out distractions while studying

30. While studying I think about many things and still get my work done

31. I find it easy to return to studying after taking a short break to clear my head

32. I have a tendency to daydream when I study

G. MOTIVATION

33. I study to learn as much as I can

34. I study to get good grades

35. I find it difficult to motivate myself to study difficult subjects

36. Getting the highest grade in class is my goal

H. MEMORY

37. To remember something, I must repeat it over and over again

38. I find it helpful to draw diagrams, outlines, etc., when trying to remember important information

	Rarely or Never	Some-times	Often or Always
39. My memory for specific facts is worse than for general concepts	_____	_____	_____
40. I use mnemonic learning devices to remember	_____	_____	_____

I. TEST-TAKING

41. I arrive late for tests	_____	_____	_____
42. I expect to do well whenever I take a test	_____	_____	_____
43. Before answering test questions I read all directions and preview the entire test	_____	_____	_____
44. I approach studying for different kinds of tests (e.g., multiple choice, true-false, essay, problem solution, etc.) in different ways	_____	_____	_____

J. MANAGING TEST ANXIETY

45. I get panicky the night before a test and have difficulty sleeping	_____	_____	_____
46. I have difficulty accepting the fact that I might not do well on every test	_____	_____	_____
47. If I get nervous during a test I am able to control it	_____	_____	_____
48. When people finish the test before me, it makes me worry and become more tense	_____	_____	_____

K. WRITING SKILLS

49. I begin working on my research papers as soon as possible to avoid end-of-the-term cramming	_____	_____	_____
50. I know how to use the library and can quickly find information that I need	_____	_____	_____

	Rarely or Never	Some-times	Often or Always
51. I follow a set format and structure when writing an essay or paper	_____	_____	_____
52. When writing I have a tendency not to footnote as much as I should	_____	_____	_____

REFERENCES

Anderson, J. (1983). A spreading activation theory of memory. *Journal of Verbal Learning and Verbal Behavior, 22,* 261-295.

Assumption College Writing Emphasis Committee. (1985). *Writing and learning: A resource book.* Unpublished document. Worcester, MA.

Atkinson, R. C., & Shiffrin, R. M. (1968). Human memory: A proposed system and its control processes. In K. W. Spence & J. T. Spence (Eds.), *The psychology of learning and motivation* (Vol. 2). New York: Academic Press.

Babkoff, H., Genser, S. G., Sing, H. C., Thorne, D., & Hegge, F. W. (1985). The effects of progressive sleep loss on a lexical decision task: Response lapses and response accuracy. *Behavior Research Methods, Instruments, & Computers, 17,* 614-622.

Baker, R. W., & Siryk, B. (1984). Measuring adjustment to college. *Journal of Counseling Psychology, 31,* 179-189.

Baker, R. W., & Siryk, B. (1989). *Student adaptation to college questionnaire manual.* Los Angeles: Western Psychological Services.

Baker, S. (1982). *The practical stylist with readings* (5th ed.). New York: Harper & Row.

Baldridge, K. P. (1979). *Seven reading strategies.* Greenwich, CT: Baldridge Reading Instruction Materials.

Bandura, A. (1977). Self-efficacy: Towards a unifying theory of human behavior. *Psychological Review, 84,* 191-215.

Bandura, A. (1982). Self-efficacy mechanism in human agency. *American Psychologist, 37,* 122-147.

Bandura, A., & Schunk, D. H. (1981). Cultivating competence, self-efficacy, and intrinsic interest through proximal self-motivation. *Journal of Personality and Social Psychology, 41,* 568-598.

Bar-Tal, D. (1978). Attributional analysis of achievement-related behavior. *Review of Educational Research, 48,* 259-271.

161

Bellezza, F. S. (1981). Mnemonic devices: Classification, characteristics and criteria. *Review of Educational Research, 51,* 247-275.

Benderson, A. (Ed.). (1989). The student writer: An endangered species? *Focus, 23,* Princeton, New Jersey: Educational Testing Service

Benware, C. A., & Deci, E. L. (1984). Quality of learning with an active versus passive motivational set. *American Educational Research Journal, 21,* 755-765.

Biehler, R. F., & Snowman, J. (1990). *Psychology applied to teaching* (6th ed.). Boston: Houghton Mifflin.

Brennan, S., Winograd, P. N., Bridge, C. A., & Hiebert, E. H. (1986). A comparison of observer reports and self-reports of study practices used by college students. *National Reading Conference Yearbook, 35,* 353-358.

Brown, A. L., Bransford, J. D., Ferrara, R. A., & Campione, J. C. (1983). Learning, remembering, and understanding. In J. H. Flavell & E. M. Markman (Eds.), *Carmichael's manual of child psychology* (Vol. 1, pp. 77-166). New York: Wiley.

Bruch, M. A., Pearl, L., & Giordano, S. (1986). Differences in the cognitive processes of academically successful and unsuccessful test anxious students. *Journal of Counseling Psychology, 33,* 217-219.

Cade, M., & Coxhead, N. (1979). *The awakened mind.* Middlesex, England: Wildwood House Limited.

Canelos, J., Dwyer, F., Taylor, W., & Nichols, R. (1984). The note-taking strategy of directed overt activity for improving learning on three types of intellectual tasks. *Journal of Instructional Psychology, 11,* 139-148.

Cautela, J., & Kastenbaum, R. (1967). A reinforcement survey schedule for use in therapy, training, and research. *Psychological Reports, 20,* 1115-1130.

Covington, M. V., & Omelich, C. L. (1987). "I knew it cold before the exam": A test of the anxiety-blockage hypothesis. *Journal of Educational Psychology, 79,* 393-400.

Craik, F. I. M., & Lockhart, R. S. (1972). Levels of processing: A framework for memory research. *Journal of Verbal Learning and Verbal Behavior, 11,* 671-684.

Cross, D. R., & Paris, S. G. (1988). Developmental and instructional analyses of children's metacognition and reading comprehension. *Journal of Educational Psychology, 80,* 131-142.

Danchise, R. A. (1985). Academic skills in the counseling center. *Journal of College Student Personnel, 26,* 245-246.

Dempster, F. N. (1987). Effects of variable encoding and spaced presentations on vocabulary learning. *Journal of Educational Psychology, 79,* 162-170.

Doan, R. E., & Scherman, A. (1987). The therapeutic effect of physical fitness on measures of personality: A literature review. *Journal of Counseling and Development, 66,* 28-36.

Dodds, J. (1986). *The writer in performance.* New York: Macmillan.

Donaghue, S. (1977). The correlation between physical fitness, absenteeism and work performance. *Canadian Journal of Public Health, 68,* 201-203.

Dweck, C. (1986). Motivational processes affecting learning. *American Psychologist, 41,* 1040-1048.

Elliott, E., & Dweck, C. (1988). Goals: An approach to motivation and achievement. *Journal of Personality and Social Psychology, 54,* 5-12.

Ellis, A., & Harper, R. (1976). *A new guide to rational living.* Hollywood, CA: Wilshire Books.

Ender, S. C. (1985). Study groups and college success. *Journal of College Student Personnel, 26,* 469-470.

Englert, C. S., Stewart, S. R., & Hiebert, E. H. (1988). Young writers' use of text structure in expository text generation. *Journal of Educational Psychology, 80,* 143-151.

Folkins, C. H., & Sine, W. E. (1981). Physical fitness training and mental health. *American Psychologist, 36,* 373-389.

Foos, P. W., & Fisher, R. P. (1988). Using tests as learning opportunities. *Journal of Educational Psychology, 80,* 179-183.

Frager, A. M. (1984). Student perceptions of school work and their effort on learning. *College Student Journal, 18,* 267-272.

Frase, L. T. (1970). Boundary conditions for mathemagenic behaviors. *Review of Educational Research, 40,* 337-347.

Galassi, J. P., Frierson, H. T., Jr., & Sharer, R. (1981). Behavior of high, moderate, and low test anxious students during an actual test situation. *Journal of Consulting and Clinical Psychology, 49,* 51-62.

George C. Gordon Library. (1985). *On-line search service.* Worcester, MA: Worcester Polytechnic Institute.

Girdano, D. A., & Girdano, D. D. (1972). *Drug education: Content and methods.* Reading, MA: Addison-Wesley.

Green, A., & Green, E. (1977). *Beyond biofeedback.* New York: Delacorte Press.

Greeno, J. G. (1978). Understanding and procedural knowledge in mathematics instruction. *Educational Psychologist, 12,* 262-283.

Gulley, J. (1988). The stages of the writing process. *Phi Delta Kappan, 69,* p. 736.

Gustafson, H. W., & Toole, D. L. (1970). Effects of adjunct questions, pretesting, and degree of student supervision on learning from instructional test. *Journal of Experimental Education, 39,* 53-58.

Hall, R. H., Rocklin, T. R., Dansereau, D. F., Skaggs, L. P., O'Donnell, A. M., Lambiotte, J. G., & Young, M. D. (1988). The role of individual differences in the cooperative learning of technical material. *Journal of Educational Psychology, 80,* 172-178.

Hamilton, R. J. (1985). A framework for the evaluation of the effectiveness of adjunct questions and objectives. *Review of Educational Research, 55,* 47-85.

Hatano, G., & Kuhara, K. (1973). Production and use of mnemonic phrases in paired-associate learning with digits as response terms. *Psychological Reports, 33,* 923-930.

Heinrichs, A. S., & LaBranche, S. P. (1986). Content analysis of 47 college learning skills textbooks. *Reading Research & Instruction, 25,* 277-287.

Horne, J. A. (1985). Sleep function, with particular reference to sleep deprivation. [Special issue: Sleep research and its clinical implications]. *Annals of Clinical Research, 17,* 199-208.

Houp, K. W., & Pearsall, T. E. (1987). *Reporting technical information* (6th ed.). New York: Macmillan.

Hult, R. E., Cohn, S., & Potter, D. (1984). An analysis of student notetaking effectiveness and learning outcome in a college lecture setting. *Journal of Instructional Psychology, 11,* 175-181.

Hunsley, J. (1985). Test anxiety, academic performance, and cognitive appraisals. *Journal of Educational Psychology, 77,* 678-682.

Hunsley, J. (1987). Cognitive processes in mathematics anxiety and test anxiety: The role of appraisals, internal dialogue, and attributions. *Journal of Educational Psychology, 79,* 388-392.

Hutchinson, M. (1986). *Megabrain.* New York: Ballantine.

Jamieson, D. W., Lydon, J. E., Stewart, G., & Zanna, M. P. (1987). Pygmalion revisited: New evidence for student expectancy effects in the classroom. *Journal of Educational Psychology, 79,* 461-466.

Jenkins, J. J. (1974). Remember that old theory of memory? Well, forget it! *American Psychologist, 29,* 785-795.

Johnson, D. W., Maruyama, G., Johnson, R., Nelson, D., & Skon, L. (1981). Effects of cooperative, competitive, and individualistic goal structures on achievement: A meta-analysis. *Psychological Bulletin, 89,* 47-62.

Kane, M. (1984). Cognitive styles of thinking and learning: II. *Academic Therapy, 20,* 83-92.

Keefer, K. E. (1969). Self-prediction of academic achievement by college students. *Journal of Educational Research, 63,* 53-56.

Kiewra, K. A. (1985). Providing the instructor's notes: An effective addition to student note taking. *Educational Psychologist, 20,* 33-39.

Kiewra, K. A. (1987). Notetaking and review: The research and its implications. *Instructional Science, 16,* 233-249.

Lack of sleep hinders ability to learn. (1989, June 25). *The Worcester Gazette,* Worcester, MA.

Leal, L. (1987). Investigation of the relation between metamemory and university students' examination performance. *Journal of Educational Psychology, 79,* 35-40.

Leo-Rhynie, E. (1985). Field independence, academic orientation, and achievement. *Current Psychological Research and Reviews, 4,* 22-27.

Levin, J. R. (1983). Pictorial strategies for school learning: Practical illustrations. In M. Pressley & J. R. Levin (Eds.), *Cognitive strategy research: Educational applications* (pp. 213-237). New York: Springer-Verlag.

Levin, J. R., Morrison, C. R., McGivern, J. E., Mastropieri, M. A., & Scruggs, T. E. (1986). Mnemonic facilitation of text-embedded science facts. *American Educational Research Journal, 23,* 489-506.

Locke, E. (1977). An empirical study of lecture notetaking among college students. *Journal of Educational Research, 77,* 93-99.

Malloch, D. C., & Michael, W. B. (1981). Predicting student grade point average. *Educational Psychology Measurement, 41,* 1127-1135.

Marsh, H. W. (1987). The big-fish-little-pond effect on academic self-concept. *Journal of Educational Psychology, 79,* 280-295.

Mayer, R. E. (1984). Aids to text comprehension. *Educational Psychologist, 19,* 30-42.

Meddis, R. (1982). Cognitive dysfunction following loss of sleep. In E. Burton (Ed.), *The pathology and psychology of cognition.* London: Methuen.

Messick, S., & Associates. (1976). *Individuality in learning.* San Francisco: Jossey-Bass.

Morgan, M. (1984). Reward-induced decrements and increments in intrinsic motivation. *Review of Educational Research, 54,* 5-30.

Morgan, M. (1985). Self-monitoring of attained subgoals in private study. *Journal of Educational Psychology, 77,* 623-630.

Morrison, T. L., Thomas, M. D., & Weaver, S. J. (1973). Self-esteem and self-estimates of academic performance. *Journal of Consulting and Clinical Psychology, 41,* 412-415.

Newman, R. G., Sansbury, D. L., & Johnson, J. M. (1976). *Improving your study skills: A programmed self-administered workbook.* Washington, DC: American University.

Novak, J. D. (1980). *Handbook for the learning how to learn program.* Ithaca: New York State College of Agriculture and Life Sciences.

Novak, J. D. & Gowin, D. B. (1984). *Learning how to learn.* London: Cambridge University Press.

Patton, J. E., Routh, D. K., & Stinard, T. A. (1986). Where do children study? Behavioral observations. *Bulletin of the Psychonometric Society, 24,* 439-440.

Peper, R. J., & Mayer, R. E. (1986). Generative effects of note-taking during science lectures. *Journal of Educational Psychology, 78,* 34-38.

Plaud, J. J., Baker, R. W., & Groccia, J. E. (1990). Freshman decidedness regarding academic major and anticipated and actual adjustment to an engineering college. *NACADA Journal, 10,* 20-26.

Reeder, G. D., McCormick, C. B., & Esselman, E. D. (1987). Self-referent processing and recall of prose. Journal of Educational Psychology, 79, 243-248.

Rickards, J. P. (1979). Adjunct postquestions in text: A critical review of methods and process. *Review of Educational Research, 49,* 181-196.

Rosenthal, N. E., Carpenter, C. J., James, S. P., Parry, B. L., Rogers, S. L. B., & Wehr, T. A. (1986). Seasonal affective disorder in children and adolescents. *American Journal of Psychiatry, 143,* 356-358.

Rosenthal, N. E., Sack, D. A., & Gillin, J. C. (1984). Seasonal affective disorder: A description of the syndrome and preliminary findings with light therapy. *Archives of General Psychiatry, 41,* 72-80.

Sagerman, N. & Mayer, R. E. (1987). Forward transfer of different reading strategies evoked by adjunct questions in science text. *Journal of Educational Psychology, 79,* 189-191.

Sarason, I. G. (Ed.). (1980). *Test anxiety: Theory, research and applications.* Hillsdale, NJ: Erlbaum.

Schneider, W. (1985). Developmental trends in the metamemory-memory behavior relationship: An integrative review. In D. L. Forrest-Pressley, G. E. McKinnon, & T. G. Waller (Eds.), *Metacognition, cognition and human performance* (pp. 57-109). New York: Academic Press.

Schuman, H., Walsh, E., Olson, C., & Etheridge, B. (1985). Effort and reward: The assumption that college grades are affected by quantity of study. *Social Forces, 63,* 945-966.

Schunk, D. H. (1981). Modeling and attributional effects on children's achievement: A self-efficacy analysis. *Journal of Educational Psychology, 73,* 93-105.

Scruggs, T. E., Mastropieri, M. A., McLoone, B. B., Levin, J. R., & Morrison, C. R. (1987). Mnemonic facilitation of learning disabled students' memory for expository prose. *Journal of Educational Psychology, 79,* 27-34.

Shenkman, H., & Cukras, G. (1986). Effects of a metacognitive study training program of underprepared college students. *National Reading Conference Yearbook, 35,* 222-226.

Sjoberg, H. (1980). Physical fitness and mental performance during and after work. *Ergonomics, 23,* 977-985.

Smith, M. A., & Baker, R. W. (1987). Freshman decidedness regarding academic major and adjustment to college. *Psychological Reports, 61,* 847-853.

Smith, R. S. (1988). *Nutrition, brain and behavior* (An annotated bibliography). (Available from R. S. Smith, Sierra Pacific Seminars, Beaverton, OR.)

Stipek, D. J., & Weisz, J. R. (1981). Perceived personal control and academic achievement. *Review of Educational Research, 51,* 101-137.

Students say cramming for exams won't make the grade. (September 29, 1987). *Newspeak.* Worcester, MA: Worcester Polytechnic Institute.

Swing, S., & Peterson, P. (1988). Elaborative and integrative thought processes in mathematics learning. *Journal of Educational Psychology, 80,* 54-66.

Tei, E., & Stewart, O. (1985). Effective studying from text: Applying metacognitive strategies. *Forum for Reading, 16,* 46-55.

Thayer, R. E. (1988). Energy walks. *Psychology Today, 22,* 12-13.

Thomas, M. H., & Dieter, J. N. (1987). The positive effect of writing practice on integration of foreign words in memory. *Journal of Educational Psychology, 79,* 249-253.

Thomas, J. W., & Rohwer, W. D., Jr. (1986). Academic studying: The role of learning strategies. *Educational Psychology, 21,* 19-41.

Tobias, S. (1987). Mandatory test review and interaction with student characteristics. *Journal of Educational Psychology, 79,* 154-161.

Tryon, G. S. (1980). The measurement and treatment of test anxiety. *Review of Educational Research, 50,* 343-372.

Tulving, E. (1983). *Elements of episodic memory.* Oxford: Clarendon Press.

Turabian, K. L. (1973). *A manual for writers of term papers, theses, and dissertations* (4th ed.). Chicago: University of Chicago Press.

University of Chicago Press. (1969). *A manual of style* (12th ed.). Chicago: Author.

University of Chicago Press. (1982). *The Chicago manual of style* (13th ed., rev.). Chicago: Author.

Ur, P. (1984). *Teaching listening comprehension.* Cambridge, England: Cambridge University Press.

U.S. Department of Health and Human Services. *Health style—a self test* (Publication No. [PHS] 81-50155). Washington, DC: Public Health Service.

Vollmer, F. (1984). Expectancy and academic achievement. *Motivation and Emotion, 8,* 67-77.

Vollmer, F. (1986). Expectancy and motivation in real life achievement situations. *British Journal of Educational Psychology, 56,* 190-196.

Wagner, D. A. (1978). Memories of Morocco: The influence of age, schooling, and environment on memory. *Cognitive Psychology, 10,* 1-28.

Webster's third new international dictionary of the English language, unabridged. (1981). Springfield, MA: Merriam-Webster.

Weiner, B. (1979). A theory of motivation for some classroom experiences. *Journal of Educational Psychology, 71,* 3-25.

Weinhold, B. K. (1987). Altered states of consciousness: Explorers guide to inner space. *Counseling and Human Development, 20,* 1-12.

Weinstein, C. E., & Mayer, R. E. (1986). The teaching of learning strategies. In M. Wittrock (Ed.), *The handbook of research on teaching.* New York: Macmillan.

Weinstein, C. E., & Rogers, B. T. (1984). *Comprehension monitoring: The neglected learning strategy.* Paper presented at the Annual Convention of the American Educational Research Association, New Orleans.

Wilson, T. D., & Linville, P. W. (1982). Improving the academic performance of college freshmen: Attribution therapy revisited. *Journal of Personality and Social Psychology, 42,* 367-376.

Wilson, T. D., & Linville, P. W. (1985). Improving the performance of college freshmen with attributional techniques. *Journal of Personality and Social Psychology, 49,* 287-293.

Winter, A., & Winter, R. (1988). *Eat right, be bright.* New York: St. Martin's Press.

Wittrock, M. C. (1974). Learning as a generative process. *Educational Psychologist, 11,* 87-95.

Wurtman, J. J. (1988). *Managing your mind and mood through food.* New York: Rawson Associates.

Wurtman, R. J., & Wurtman, J. J. (Eds.). (1986). *Nutrition and the brain* (Vol. 7). New York: Raven Press.

BIBLIOGRAPHY

Part 1. A Selected Guide to Resources for Research Papers and Writing Assignments

Guidebooks on How to Use Library Reference Sources

These general sources are excellent starting points for library research. They usually include sections on: How to find information, how to trace books, and listing of reference sources by subject and discipline. Each contains annotated descriptions of sources.

Chandler, G. (1982). *How to find out: Printed and on-line sources* (5th ed.). Oxford, England: Pergamon Press.

Cheney, F. N., & Williams, W. J. (1980). *Fundamental reference sources* (2nd ed.). Chicago: American History Association.

Hillard, J. M. (1984). *Where to find what: A handbook to reference service.* Metuchen, NJ: Scarecrow Press.

O'Brien, R., & Soderman, J. (1974). *The basic guide to research sources.* New York: Mentor.

General Bibliographies and Indexes

A great place to start. From here you can locate sources for more in-depth information.

Access: The supplemental guide to periodicals.
(1975). Syracuse, NY: Gaylord.
Lists nontechnical and popular periodicals not in *The readers guide to periodical literature.*

Bibliographic Index, 1937-present.
New York: Wilson.
Includes bibliographies published as parts of books and those published separately.

Computerized Bibliographies
Check with your reference librarians. There are different kinds,

some free and some that charge a fee. See "Selected On-Line Search Data Bases."

Essay and General Literature Index,
    1900-present. New York: Wilson.
    Guide to literary essays found in books and anthologies.

Government Reports Announcements and Index.
    Indexes U.S. government-sponsored research in all subject areas.

Humanities Index, 1974-present.
    New York: Wilson.
    Use if subject relates to art, architecture, folklore, history, language, literature, philosophy, or religion.

National Technical Information Service (NTIS), 1964-present. Indexes references to U.S. government-sponsored research reports.

The Reader's Guide to Periodical Literature, 1900-present. New York: Wilson. Indexes articles from magazines intended for general, not professional, readership.

Sheehy, E. P. (1968). *Guide to reference books.*
    Chicago: American Library Association.
    An excellent general guide to reference materials.

Social Sciences Index, 1974-present.
    New York: Wilson.
    Indexes scholarly articles in anthropology, economics, environmental science, education, law, medicine, political science, psychology, and sociology.

Abstracting Services

These sources provide brief summaries of sources. Helpful for quickly finding out about many resources without actually looking them up individually.

Abstracts in Anthropology, 1970-present.

Biology Abstracts, 1926-present.

Chemical Abstracts, 1907-present.

Child Development Abstracts and Bibliography, 1924-present.

Dissertation Abstracts

Energy Research Abstracts
  U.S. Dept. of Energy report literature as well as other federal government energy research summarized.

Historical Abstracts, 1777-1945.
  Abstracts articles on world history.

INIS Atomindex
  Abstracts of international nuclear report literature.

Language and Language Behavior, 1967-present.

Psychological Abstracts, 1927-present.

Sociological Abstracts, 1953-present.

Book Reviews

Book Review Digest, 1905-present.
  The primary resource for locating book reviews.

Book Review Index, 1965-present.
  Indexes reviews in scholarly journals and art magazines.

Technical Book Review Index, current.

Government Publications

Congressional Information Service/Index.
  Indexes U.S. congressional publications (except Congressional Record).

Congressional Record Index.
  Indexes daily record of U.S. Congress.

Monthly Catalog of United States Government Publications.
  Excellent subject index.

Subject Indexes

Art:

    Art Index, 1964-present.

Biography:

    Biography Index, 1946-present.

    Current Biography, 1945-present.

Business:

    Business Index
    Microfilm index to 375 magazines.

    Business Periodicals Index, 1958-present.

Education:

    Current Index to Journals in Education, 1969-present.

    Education Index, 1929-present.

History:

    America: History and Life. A Guide to Periodical Literature, 1964-present.

    International Bibliography of Historical Sciences, 1930-present.

    Writings on American History, 1902-present.

Language & Literature:

    The Critical Index: A Bibliography of Film, 1946-73.

    Essay and General Literature Index, 1900-present.

    International Bibliography, 1922-present.

    M.L.A. Bibliography, 1921-present.
    Deals with articles concerning all modern languages.

Play Index, 1949-1982.

Speech Index

Law:

 Index to Legal Periodicals, 1952-present.

 Legal Resource Index.
 Microfilm listing of over 600 newspapers and magazines.

Library Science:

 Library Literature, 1921-present.

Mathematics:

 Mathematical Reviews, 1968-1978.

Medicine:

 Abridged Index Medicus, 1970-present.

Music:

 Music Index, 1949-present.

Nursing:

 International Nursing Index, 1966-present.

 Nursing and Allied Health Index, 1956-present.

Philosophy and Religion:

 Philosopher's Index, 1967-present.

Political Science:

 Political Science: A Bibliographic Guide to the Literature,
 1965 and 1974.

Public Affairs:

 Public Affairs Information Service Bulletin (P.A.I.S.), 1915-present.
 Excellent guide to all social sciences as well.

Quotations:

Bartlett, J. (1968). *Familiar quotations.*

Science:

Applied Science and Technology Index, 1958-present.

Biological and Agricultural Index, 1964-present.

General Science Index, 1978-present.

SAE Transactions Index-Abstracts
Index of all technical papers issued by the Society of Automotive
Engineers.

Science and Engineering References Sources, 1967-present.

Scientific and Technical Aerospace Reports, 1962-present.

Statistics:

*American Statistics Index: A Comprehensive Guide to the Statistical
Publications of the United States Government,* 1973-present.
Includes abstracts.

The Gallup Opinion Index: Political, Social and Economic Trends,
1965-present.

Statistical Abstract of the United States, 1878-present.
Includes summaries of social, political, economic and cultural data.

Statistical Yearbook, 1949-present.

World Almanac, current.

Part 2. Selected On-Line Search Data Bases

There are presently more than 200 data bases to which college libraries
have access. These often correspond to printed indexes in nearly every
subject area. Your research topic will determine which data base will be
searched. Check with your library's on-line search consultant to find out
which data bases are available to you. Examples of available on-line data
bases are:

Engineering:

COMPENDEX — All engineering disciplines
NTIS — U.S. government research and development reports
STANDARDS AND SPECIFICATIONS

Humanities:

AMERICA: HISTORY AND LIFE — history
HISTORICAL ABSTRACTS — history
MLA BIBLIOGRAPHY — language, literature

Science:

BIOSIS — biology
CHEMICAL ABSTRACTS — chemistry
ENVIROLINE — environment, pollution
INSPEC — physics, electrical engineering, computers
MATHFILE — mathematics
MEDLINE — medicine and related areas
SCISEARCH — Science Citation Index

Social Sciences:

ERIC — education
HARVARD BUSINESS REVIEW — business, economics and related
 areas
MANAGEMENT CONTENTS — management
PAIS — public affairs, policy studies, social sciences
SOCIOLOGICAL ABSTRACTS — sociology

Part 3. A Selected Listing of Writing Style Guides

American Psychological Association. (1983). *Publication manual of the American Psychological Association. Washington, DC: Author.*

Modern Languages Association. (1979). *MLA handbook for writers of research papers, theses, and dissertations.* New York: Author.

Turabian, K. L. (1973). *A manual for writers of term papers, theses, and dissertations* (4th ed.). Chicago: University of Chicago Press. The most widely used writing source on college campuses today.

University of Chicago Press. (1982). *The Chicago manual of style* (13th ed., rev.). Chicago: Author.